TERENCE CONRAN
STORAGE
GET ORGANIZED

Author's Note

Please, please do read this book as well as, I hope, being inspired by the pictures. Elizabeth Wilhide and I have a great deal of experience and knowledge about home design and how to organize the chaotic aspects of household clutter that can often spoil the enjoyment of your home. Our collective knowledge is all here.

My thanks to Liz Boyd who researched the pictures, Zia Mattocks who edited the book and Lucy Gowans who designed it. And, of course, thanks to Elizabeth Wilhide, who has worked so happily with me on many books, and to Nu-Nu Yee, my PA, the tidiest, neatest and best-organized person I've ever met.

Published in 2006 by Conran Octopus Limited
a part of the Octopus Publishing Group
2–4 Heron Quays, London E14 4JP
www.conran-octopus.co.uk

Distributed in the United States and Canada by
Sterling Publishing Co., Inc.
387 Park Avenue South, New York, NY 10016-8810

ISBN-13: 978-1-84091-434-4
ISBN-10: 1-84091-434-3

Printed in China

Consultant Editor Elizabeth Wilhide
Publishing Director Lorraine Dickey
Executive Editor Zia Mattocks
Art Director Jonathan Christie
Art Editor Lucy Gowans
Picture Research Manager Liz Boyd
Production Manager Angela Young

CONTENTS

Introduction

OPPOSITE: This apartment in Japan reveals a rather novel and idiosyncratic approach to organizing one's belongings, with all the paraphernalia of everyday life stowed in the compartments that honeycomb the walls.

Once, during an interview in Japan, I was asked what would be the single most important piece of advice I could give to people about their homes. My answer was to say that when the time came to redecorate, people should take all their possessions outside into the garden, put them under a tarpaulin and bring back into the house only those things they needed or truly loved. Nothing I have ever said before or since has had such an impact on an audience. It's not surprising – while space is in very short supply in Japan, gift-giving is a very important part of the culture, and many homes are consequently very cluttered. Even so, I was amazed at the response.

That same watershed moment came for me a year or so ago when the boiler blew up at my house in the country. Faced with major disruption, we decided to take the opportunity to redo the bathrooms

at the same time. Then, while everything was upside down, we also began a major clearout. We managed to dispose of quite a few things. We sold some, donated others and threw out what was unusable. Of the remainder, there were still quite a number of items that I wanted to hang on to, but which were silting up the house and generally merited being retired from view for a while. Luckily, the house has a large cellar that had previously been used, fairly haphazardly, as an all-purpose dumping ground. I cleaned out one of the big basement rooms, whitewashed the walls, put in a good industrial double-sided racking system and installed a few dehumidifiers. Then I packed up those things that I didn't want to dispose of and put them into boxes and stored them down there. The difference in atmosphere throughout the entire house was immediately apparent, and rooms that had been

getting rather stale became much more uplifting places to be. Since then, however, some of the boxes have been opened and various things have started trickling back upstairs again …

I have to admit I find it difficult at times to get rid of things, despite the positive effect dejunking has on the quality and quantity of space. For example, as a war child, I can't bear to see food thrown away. Once you have experienced extreme shortages during your formative years, it's very difficult to rid yourself of this sort of attitude. But the war years were also instructive on the perils of hoarding. At the beginning of the Second World War my mother, guessing correctly that sweets (candy) would be virtually unobtainable, filled several large jars with humbugs and other boiled sweets (hard candy) – every child's sugary dream. Those sweets stayed in the jars all through the war, and we were never allowed to have one. Finally, on VE Day, my mother judged it was an appropriate time for celebration. Of course, by then the sweets were all congealed and inedible.

You may well not have a stockpile of ancient boiled sweets sitting around in your home, but most of us share our lives with other belongings that are clearly redundant, sometimes embarrassingly so. While it does take a certain degree of time and effort to dispose of things, I suspect much of our reluctance to part with our belongings can be put down to the fact that we feel we are wasting money by getting rid of possessions that we once paid for, even if those possessions are worn out, broken or simply not needed any more. In this respect, it can be useful to consider the cost of your home in monetary terms. Every square foot has a value when you take into account the mortgage and other overheads that you pay, such as local rates and utility bills.

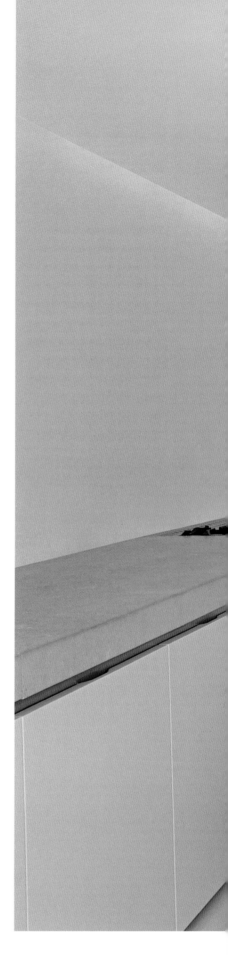

What is worth more: the space itself, or the broken lawnmower that you are never going to fix or the box of wedding presents that you don't like?

Getting organized is one thing; staying organized is necessarily a fairly constant process. To aid you in the former task, this book contains advice on storage systems and strategies, from built-in or fitted solutions, such as closets and cupboards, to containers and display. When I used to run Habitat, our branches in France sold masses of laminated cardboard boxes with metal edging that were made for us in Sweden. The same containers barely sold at all in the UK. I don't precisely know what that says about the different approach to storage in the two countries, but I do know that buying more things is not always the answer to storage problems. In this respect, I also remember encountering a woman racing around our old shop in Manhattan, snatching up various storage-related items. 'This morning I woke up and decided it was time to get organized!' she exclaimed. While I was happy to see her buying our products so enthusiastically, I had a sneaking suspicion that she might have been going about it the wrong way round. For that reason, this book also covers basic routines and approaches that will enable you to keep on top of clutter in the future by tackling the problem at source.

That is not to say you need to be rigidly disciplined to enjoy the benefits of good organization. The late Hugh Casson told me once about a visit he had made to Philip Johnson in his Glass House in Connecticut. During the course of their conversation, the architect had gone over to a concealed

RIGHT: The British architect John Pawson is internationally renowned as an advocate of minimalism. His London home clearly demonstrates his mastery of the Zen notion of 'thinglessness'.

cupboard, extracted a book and given it to Hugh to look at while he left the room. When Hugh finished leafing through the book, he was at a complete loss where to put it down in the seamless minimal interior. Eventually, he laid it neatly in the very centre of a glass table. A little while later, Johnson came back into the room and, with a frown of irritation, retrieved the book and stowed it back in the cupboard. I enjoy the serenity of uncluttered space, but perhaps that's taking things too far.

Our relationship with the things we own can be complicated and surprisingly emotional. When possessions threaten to take over, however, it is not only daily routines that suffer, but also our fundamental enjoyment of our homes. Get organized and you will be able to tackle essential chores much more practically and effectively, and at the same time derive real pleasure from your surroundings.

PLANNING AND ASSESSMENT

1. Creative Review

The starting point when it comes to tackling storage needs, whether on a greater or lesser scale, is to review what you own and how it is kept. Significant points of transition, such as moving house or major redecorating or remodelling, are naturally good times for wholehearted reassessment. When you have to clear the living room so that it can be painted, it's the perfect opportunity to take the time to sort through your books or CD collection. When you are moving to a new home, it makes sense to cast a critical eye over your belongings and think carefully about what you intend to take with you. Changes of personal circumstance – setting up home for the first time, becoming a family or launching a business from home – are also ideal times for careful rethinking. Otherwise, you may be inspired to get to grips with your possessions when you are suddenly faced with a major overspill: books that can't be shelved because you have run out of shelf space; drawers that won't close because too much is stuffed inside them. When it comes to home organization, it is best to accept that the process of review is fairly ongoing.

OPPOSITE: These are a few of my favourite objects that I keep on display at my house in the country. Whatever things you have on view in your home should give you pleasure, not serve as a niggling reminder of a chore left undone.

ABOVE: It is always important to consider access when you are stowing belongings in out-of-the-way locations. This simple ladder provides a means of reaching a high-level storage area.

KEY STAGES

Different stages of life throw up unique organizational challenges. We acquire belongings at varying rates according to our present needs and circumstances, and each new period offers an opportunity for re-evaluation. Some stages in life are more dramatic and far-reaching in their effects than others – for example, moving in with a partner when your belongings effectively double, or starting a new family. All, however, provide natural transition points for reviewing what you own and how you keep it.

First home

As soon as you move into your first home, you are likely to meet the whole issue of storage head-on. Most first homes, whether they are rented or the first step onto the property ladder, tend to be on the small side, which means that you are automatically starting with a basic shortfall of space to put things. This is all the more acute if you are sharing your accommodation with friends or if you are moving in with your partner. Looking on the bright side, however, this also tends to be a stage in life when people haven't yet accumulated serious amounts of extraneous baggage.

When grown children set up their first permanent home, this often provides a clear signal to their parents to clear out the emptying nest. All those relics and mementoes of your schooldays and childhood may suddenly become your responsibility to look after, particularly if your parents have designs on your old room. Setting up your first home provides an ideal opportunity to make a final decision about those belongings that have lingered on in your old

family home as nostalgic markers of previous years. If your parents have enough room, the items that you want to keep can be boxed up and stored in an out-of-the-way location until you can give them a permanent home yourself.

If you are short of money as well as space, you may find that family and friends offer you a motley collection of furniture and other bits and pieces to help get you started. This is all well and good if the items in question are useful and what you want in the first place, but just another form of overload if they are not. Resist the temptation to become the means by which other people shed their unwanted possessions.

If you are part of a couple setting up home for the first time – unless your relationship has a question mark hanging over its future – now is the time to pool your possessions and dispose of duplicate items. You may want to hang on to your own copy of a favourite novel, but there is really no reason, for example, to give two can openers houseroom. Keep the one that works best, is newest or is of better quality, and get rid of the other.

Points to consider:

• Built-in or fitted storage, preferably concealed for a more streamlined finish, makes the most of limited and awkward space. Rather than buy a number of individual items of storage furniture, which eat up floor area and are visually distracting, spend the same money on putting up shelves and building cupboards.

• Think about hiring off-site storage facilities for any possessions that you don't have room for at the present time, but would like to retain for future use.

• When you set up home for the first time with another person, you are bound to encounter differences in basic attitudes to possessions and their means of organization. If these issues are not to become a battleground, it is best to try to arrange matters so that each of you has some personal space for your own playground.

• If you are spending quite a large proportion of time away from home – at work during the day and socializing at night – clutter can soon creep up on you. Try to build in some time during the week when you can tackle household matters and put things straight before it becomes an overwhelming and time-consuming task.

Family home

Family life brings with it rapid changes on all fronts. As children grow, develop interests and embark on their schooling, the type and number of possessions that support such activities will change and proliferate, almost exponentially at times. For most people, this is a critical period when it comes to maintaining systems of home organization that are both flexible and workable. Keeping on top of burgeoning clutter also means that your clearout sessions will need to be more frequent and more thorough.

It is all very well to suggest that you exercise a degree of restraint when it comes to acquiring possessions at this stage of life: in practice, it is virtually impossible. Nor is it entirely desirable. While children do not need showers of material goods to know that they are loved or to develop emotionally, intellectually or physically, all parents like to provide their children with the things that they want as well as the things they need. It simply goes along with the nurturing role. That is not to say that you should give in to 'pester power' (although most of us do, at least from time to time); it is merely that you will have to accept that this stage of life is inevitably a time of more, rather than less.

Children grow so fast in all respects that it is not difficult to find natural transition points for reviewing possessions and storage needs. Each successive stage of development is marked by the redundancy of the previous stage's clothing, toys, books, games, and so on. Even furniture and equipment falls into this category as cots or cribs give way to beds or bunks, and highchairs, buggies and strollers are no longer required. While there may be treasured items you will want to keep to mark your child's progress – or to hand down to siblings or future generations – fairly swift turnarounds at regular intervals are generally essential. As children grow older, expect them to have their own views on what is kept and what is not, which will call for some sensitivity and diplomacy.

Just as important is the need to set up a system of organization that supports your daily routine. This should be neither so rigid that it becomes a bone of contention nor so fluid that you stand no chance of finding anything at all. It doesn't matter that the red Lego is mixed up with the other colours, or that the felt-tip pens are in the same box as the crayons; it does matter if important documents go missing, homework is lost and no one can find the first-aid kit when a cut knee needs bandaging.

Children are more likely to flourish if they are brought up in surroundings that are calm and reasonably orderly. While they may well be the biggest creators of mess in the first place, they will learn to treat belongings (both theirs and yours) with a greater degree of respect if there is the means to do so and a clear example for them to follow. This means providing accessible forms of storage that they can reach, such as containers, baskets and low-level shelves. It also means refusing to accept that mess is an inevitable accompaniment to family life. Managing a household with young children, especially where there are adult careers to juggle, takes a great deal of energy, and it can be tempting to let things slide a little. Whatever time you save by not tidying up, however, will be more than spent on another occasion when you come to look for things and can't find them.

ABOVE: This family kitchen achieves a good balance between open display areas, where the more attractive items of kitchen equipment are kept, and closed cupboards for essential but less visually appealing supplies and accessories. Bear in mind, however, that whatever is kept out on view in a kitchen will need to be washed frequently.

Points to consider:

• Instigate regular clearout sessions to keep on top of whatever is outgrown or surplus to requirements. This is equally applicable to adult possessions.

• Think about rotating belongings in and out of deep storage according to seasonal requirements. Pack away winter clothes and sports gear in attics, basements, garages and similar remote locations in the summer, and vice versa. Deep storage is also useful for items that are required only once or twice a year, such as Christmas decorations.

• Modular storage containers can be a good way of organizing children's games, puzzles and art supplies, as well as CD, video and DVD collections.

• Working walls of storage in hallways, where the wall is lined with shelves or cupboards, or a combination of the two, can help to keep main living areas free of extraneous mess.

• As soon as children are old enough, enlist their help in tidying up. Don't attempt to enforce a standard of order they have no hope of achieving, but don't succumb to chaos, either.

• Assign dedicated places for important documentation (birth certificates, records of immunization, and so on), as well as emergency items such as fuses, light bulbs and the first-aid box.

• Most children treasure their artwork and models. Paintings and pictures are easy enough to store in folders, but large-scale endeavours can start to take over. After a decent time has elapsed in which such creations have been fully appreciated in all their glory, one way of disposing of them without upsetting the child is to photograph them and stick the pictures into an album or workbook – it's either that or continue to share your home with a menagerie or flotilla made of cereal boxes and empty toilet rolls.

Home business

Most people do at least some (paid) work away from the office over the course of their careers, but if you take the plunge and decide to base yourself exclusively at home you will inevitably face an additional organizational challenge. The systems and arrangements you may already have in place for dealing with routine household administration will not be adequate to cope with the demands of running a business efficiently and profitably.

Much, of course, will depend on the nature of your home business. If your work is largely desk- and computer-based, you will require additional storage for paperwork, files, documentation and reference material. If you are producing goods for sale, you will need dedicated areas to store supplies, equipment and completed articles prior to dispatch.

Unless you have a workshop, garage, shed or adjacent outbuilding that can be adopted as a base for your business, it is likely that you will need more than a single storage area to serve your working needs: perhaps storage in the immediate vicinity of your desk; shelves or filing cabinets relatively nearby for recent archives and files; and remote or deep storage for the type of documentation which you need to keep for legal or tax purposes. In Britain, for example, income tax returns must by law be kept for seven years.

Points to consider:

• Is there room to grow? The longer you run your business or career from home, the more space you will require to keep essential records relating to your working history. Periodic clearouts will only go so far: expect to accumulate.

• When you have made the decision to work from home, spend some time planning your systems of organization so that the visual effect is neat, unobtrusive and well considered, rather than an ad hoc arrangement of box files, filing cabinets and disparate storage containers. When your working space is also your home, appearances matter.

ABOVE: A mezzanine level in this spacious and light-filled Australian home doubles up as a dining area and workspace. Low-level shelving tucked under the slope of the roof houses a collection of books. The flexible space is simply furnished with an easy-going combination of old and new pieces.

Empty nest

As someone who has been through the experience more often than most, I often joke that there's nothing like a divorce for instigating a good clearout. I remember after one of my divorces moving into a new place with only the contents of a tea chest and a suitcase. Unfortunately, when I later came to move out, that tea chest and suitcase had expanded to four pantechnicons' worth of belongings.

Joking aside, there is inevitably a stage in family life when the home begins to empty. Children grow and leave home to start lives of their own, and some can even be persuaded to take their possessions with them. The painful ruptures of divorce and bereavement inevitably have their own dramatic impact on domestic arrangements.

As anyone who has weathered this stage of life can tell you, it is a natural time for reassessment, not only of what you own, but also of the way you use the space at your disposal. As well as making practical sense, reorganization can help you to look to the future in a positive light, rather than wistfully lingering over memories of the days when your children were young and running you ragged.

Family homes, however, empty at differing rates. In some households, the period may be quite protracted. When your children are at college or university, it can be a particularly testing time – one minute, you are decanting most of the contents of their bedroom at home into a student house or room in a hall of residence; the next, you are bringing twice as much back home. It is as well to accept the fact that for some years there will be a bit of a boomerang effect, as possessions shuttle backwards and forwards between different locations.

One further complication of this stage can arise with the death of your parents or in-laws, and the need to decide which of their possessions, family records, photographs and mementoes to add to your collection. Family history is important to all of us as a reminder of continuity, as well as of special times. There is a difference, however, between cherishing a few significant items from the past and turning your home into what amounts to an archive or museum.

Points to consider:

• During the college or university years, reduce the strain on your back and your living space by investigating whether there are any arrangements for storing students' belongings out of term time. Many colleges provide storage rooms where boxes and bulky items can be left over the vacations.

• Once your children have left home for good, insist that they take as many of their belongings with them as they can. Mementoes and other items they wish to keep but do not have room for can go into deep storage, or into a rented storage facility.

• Be discriminating when it comes to clearing the homes of your elderly or deceased relatives. In terms of furniture and furnishings, think about whether you actually like the item in question enough to give it houseroom and whether it will fit with your other pieces. Share out records and photographs relating to family history with other family members.

• Rethink the way you use your home once a bedroom or two has become available. Now is a good time to make radical alterations to spatial planning.

OPPOSITE: Neutral zones, such as corridors and landings, can be fitted out as storage areas, provided there is sufficient room left over for people to get from place to place easily. This wall storage system provides a neat and unobtrusive combination of open and closed compartments.

HOW TO IDENTIFY CLUTTER

Clutter, rather like comfort, is inevitably something of a subjective notion. While I tend to be a 'less is more' sort of person, I am no minimalist, and am not content to gaze upon uniformly empty walls and echoing space. On the other hand, I accept that some people do prefer to surround themselves with rather more belongings than I would be happy to share my life with on a daily basis.

Nevertheless, there are times in everyone's life when possessions threaten to compromise our use and enjoyment of our homes. If clutter might be defined as those belongings that are redundant or that serve no useful purpose, it might also be seen as an ongoing pending file of jobs not yet done – paperwork that remains to be dealt with, drawers that need to be sorted through, items requiring a decision on whether they should be kept, repaired or disposed of, as well as those things that are perpetually in orbit and lack a settled home.

When this type of clutter builds up, it can not only begin to hinder your ability to carry out ordinary routines efficiently – you won't be able to find things you need, for a start – but it can also produce a curiously draining effect on your will to tackle anything at all. I am not an especial believer in feng shui; neither am I seeking any great psychological meaning in all of this. Yet it seems obvious that when dozens of such organizational chores are niggling away at you – and you are doing your best to ignore them – the result can easily be an encroaching sense of frustrated stagnation, as if you were living in a fog. When clutter is obscuring the picture, you will naturally lose focus and concentration.

When various places around the home are being inappropriately used as interim storage areas, it is a telltale sign that clutter is gaining the upper hand. A hall table that is disappearing under unsorted letters; chairs and sofas piled with books or papers; stairs that are gathering a collection of disparate belongings waiting a trip up or down to the next level – all indicate basic shortfalls in organization and decision-making. Another symptom is where the same basic type of possession is being stored in a number of different places throughout the home: in most cases, it generally makes sense to provide one dedicated place to keep items of a similar nature, rather than several scattered ones.

Extreme cases of clutter make good reality TV, where 'clutter consultants' descend on a household and help untie psychological knots while throwing out the junk. Most of us, however, do not let things get so out of hand that we need professional help. Even so, it is as well to be aware that dejunking can be a surprisingly emotional process. To begin with, getting to grips with clutter requires making a series of decisions – Is it worth saving? Is it worth mending? Where best to put it? – which can feel rather relentless and overwhelming. Then again, sifting through possessions

ABOVE: If the framework of shelving is very strong, it helps to provide a sense of cohesion and order, so that what is displayed on the shelves reads as one collection. Here, the vertical supports are strongly expressed, while the shelves themselves are less noticeable.

OPPOSITE: A generous bathroom converted from a former bedroom – and complete with fireplace – deserves to be treated as a room first and a functional area second. The 'living' aspect of things is kept to the fore by discreet fitted storage for bathroom essentials such as towels and spare toiletries. Those items deserving to be on view are kept in a glass-fronted cabinet.
RIGHT: Subdivided drawers and trays – such as this printer's tray – can be used to display a collection of similar objects. Stowing things into boxes or compartments has intrinsic appeal.

inevitably stirs up memories and expectations, which force you to re-evaluate your life in terms of the present, rather than hold on to the past. Guilt-making reminders of former enthusiasms or good intentions that fizzled out or came to nothing can prove just as hard to discard as sentimental mementoes of family life or personal achievements. Getting rid of expensive or emotional possessions – even if they are broken, worn out or don't fit – can also be very difficult.

While clutter is not conducive to a relaxed or productive frame of mind, it has other deleterious effects on your physical surroundings and wellbeing. If one particular area in your home is serving as a repository for unfinished business, or a catch-all for possessions that you have not got round to deciding what to do with, the chances are it won't have been cleaned regularly or thoroughly. If the cubbyhole under the stairs is stuffed with unopened boxes from your last house move, it will be difficult to vacuum and dust effectively. In this context, dejunking can have an immediate effect on air quality by opening up areas that were formerly blocked, and allowing breezes to circulate. Similarly, a wardrobe, closet or clothes rail that is stuffed to bursting point provides ideal conditions for moths to proliferate and decimate your clothes, while overfilled refrigerators will not be able to operate effectively, which means that food might not be as chilled as it should be.

Clutter also dramatically increases the time and effort you need to locate things. If you have to battle through the box room or storage closet to find the spare duvet, it adds an additional layer of difficulty and vexation to the task. If you have to search the whole house, top to bottom, for an article that has never had a fixed keeping place, chances are you will end up buying another sooner or later. Duplicate, or triplicate, items often come into the home this way and represent a direct waste of money.

By far the most wasteful effect of clutter, however, is the most obvious, and that is the fact that it devours space. Nothing in this day and age is more valuable, and the property pages prove it. No matter what size your home is, if you proceed to fill it up with meaningless clutter, you might as well be paying a premium to live in a shoebox.

What to get rid of

Possessions come in so many different forms – from your child's first drawings to pots and pans, from Christmas decorations to income tax returns – that it is difficult to come up with a cut-and-dried rule that could be applied across the board and enable you to distinguish what is necessary from what is redundant. Nevertheless, there are a few guidelines that should enable you to determine areas of your life where clutter is building up and which items, broadly speaking, you should think about getting rid of.

• Any practical item, including clothing, that you have not used or worn for over a year should be considered ripe for disposal. Many kitchen gadgets fall into this category, particularly specific pieces of equipment that reflect a short-lived enthusiasm for a particular type of cooking or a well-intentioned determination to bake bread or make pasta or ice cream that has not quite materialized.
• Most duplicate items, including CDs, books, kitchen equipment and garden tools. Exceptions include certain articles, such as scissors, which you may want to keep on hand in different areas of the home.
• Any item or piece of equipment that has been awaiting mending or repair for more than a few months. If you have managed without it for a considerable period of time, chances are you do not really need it.
• Any possession that induces guilt. This is a wide-ranging category and includes clothing that doesn't fit or suit you; impulse buys or 'bargains' you regretted almost as soon as you left the store; books you have never got round to reading (ditto CDs, videos and DVDs); and gifts that you don't like or haven't a use for.
• Anything that you are keeping on the off chance that it might either come in useful or become valuable one day. What is more useful and more valuable is the space that it is occupying.
• Equipment, materials or supplies that relate to activities, such as hobbies or sports, that you no longer pursue – or have never quite got round to taking up.
• Old magazines, newspapers and any other old papers or files that you are not required to keep by law or to maintain your career.
• Many of us have blind spots with respect to clearly redundant items, which nevertheless linger on in cupboards and drawers.

These include: old cosmetics and medicines; old paint, chemicals and insecticides; accessories and manuals relating to equipment that has since been replaced.
• Anything that has not been unpacked since you moved in.

How to prevent clutter from accumulating

Once you have got rid of redundant items (see pages 34–7 for methods of disposal) and restored order to your home, the benefits will be immediately apparent in an increased sense of space and a more relaxed and productive atmosphere, not to mention in your own glow of satisfaction. How to keep things that way?

• Most people, excepting the chronically chaotic, have particular areas of their lives where clutter tends to build up. For some, it is clothing which causes the difficulty; for others, it is paperwork. Know your weakness and resolve to keep on top of things.
• Sort through different categories of possessions at regular intervals (weekly, monthly, seasonally or yearly). Weekly is not too often for newspapers; seasonally is generally adequate for adult clothing, whereas monthly is more appropriate for children in growing spurts.
• Make it easy to recycle or 'dejunk'. Dedicated recycling boxes help you to dispose of household waste effectively and responsibly.
• Make use of the natural urge to turn a new leaf that comes in spring. If you wake up in the mood to get to grips with your wardrobe or filing cabinet, act on it.
• Review the way you shop. If you find yourself constantly throwing out food that is past its use-by date, your shopping list is not attuned to your present eating habits. If you know yourself to be an inveterate accumulator of non-essential items or someone who is unable to resist a bargain, cut down on the opportunities you have to provide yourself with something you don't need and haven't got room for.
• Take the time to return things to their proper homes after use.

OPPOSITE: Ridding yourself of unnecessary clutter provides more space to display the things that really give you pleasure. This display wall is well lit by natural light from the windows set into the plane of the roof.

LEFT: Old or reclaimed items of storage furniture often have years of useful life left in them. An unfitted approach to kitchen storage works particularly well in older properties or in country locations, where the traditional kitchen dresser (hutch) has long reigned supreme.

OPPOSITE: A working wall of storage systemizes a considerable number of shelvable belongings. The staircase offers a convenient means of access to the higher shelves.

MEANS OF DISPOSAL

Ideally, as little time as possible should elapse between your decision to get rid of something and its physical removal from your home. This ensures both that you run no risk of changing your mind and that the redundant item does not remain sitting around in limbo.

There is something exhilarating about filling up plastic sacks with unwanted belongings and putting them out with the trash. Even more joyful is a good bonfire in the garden. Nevertheless, while both disposal methods are virtually instant, they are also intrinsically wasteful for all but the most perished or unusable things. Kinder to the environment – and occasionally to your wallet – are a number of other outlets, from recycling centres to auction houses. Don't clear out your home at the expense of adding to already overburdened landfill sites – it is estimated that Londoners alone generate 17 million tonnes of waste annually.

Making donations

A popular means of disposal of unwanted goods is to donate them to charity. Such outlets include shops, sales at your local church or school, and neighbourhood schemes selling unwanted furniture and appliances to people on low incomes. Your donations will find a new home, and the charity in question will make money for its good cause.

Many charity shops will take a wide range of items including clothing, toys and games, books and ornaments. Make sure that what you donate is clean and in reasonably good condition – jigsaw puzzles and games should include all the pieces; crockery and glassware should be unchipped; and clothing should be undamaged by stains, tears and moths. Your urge to get rid of your clutter may be strong, but do not rush down to the charity shop with your bags and boxes when the shop is not open. Donations left on the doorstep may be drenched or scattered all over the street. And don't give away what no one would want.

Bulkier items can be more difficult to dispose of. However, many local areas now run recycling projects for furniture, selling pieces on through non-profit-making stores at affordable prices. Many such schemes will collect your unwanted goods for free, or charge you only a small donation, which is definitely more cost-effective than paying either the council or a haulier to come and cart it away for you and much better for the environment, too. Furniture has to be in good condition and may have to comply with fire regulations. Similarly, appliance reuse centres will collect working electrical appliances – everything from refrigerators to microwaves – test them and sell them at vastly reduced prices with a six-month guarantee.

Local hospitals, clinics, libraries and schools may also be glad of your donations. Some areas run toy libraries, for example, or you may find hospital crèches or children's wards would be grateful for the toys your children have grown out of. Similarly, books and CDs may be donated to local libraries or schools, and magazines to doctors' or dental surgeries.

LEFT: Old school lockers, stripped of their paint to reveal the glossy steel finish, make practical cubbyholes for children's toys and books. A clear varnish will keep the exposed metal from rusting.

BELOW: Wooden drawers in the base of this built-in bench seat provide additional discreet storage space in a living area. Deep drawers should be easy to pull out and not overloaded with heavy items.

Recycling

Recycling schemes have grown increasingly prevalent in recent years, and many areas now offer a home collection service in addition to providing centrally located recycling banks. In some parts of the world it is a legal requirement that all household waste must be separated into different categories, then recycled. Standard recycled goods include paper, bottles (clear, green and brown) and cans (steel and aluminium). Clothing and shoe banks are also becoming more common.

A relatively new manifestation of recycling comes in the form of Internet swapshops or exchanges. Some of these websites are specifically geared to a particular category of goods – for example, designer clothing – while others are more inclusive. The idea is that you exchange whatever things you don't want for something else that you do. Such schemes can also be a good way of disposing of unwanted electronic items such as old mobile (cell) phones.

ABOVE: Reviewing your wardrobe on a regular basis will prevent it from turning into source of guilt and frustration. Most people wear only a small proportion of the clothing they own, which represents a direct waste of space.

Selling

Parting company with your possessions can be a little less painful if you know you are going to make some money or make somebody happy in the process. Of course, it works both ways, and the reason why some people find it difficult to dispose of clearly redundant items is that they believe they will be valuable one day.

When it comes to selling there are numerous routes you can take, depending on what you are intending to dispose of. If you are unsure about whether an item is valuable, you may need an expert opinion from an auction house or dealer. The last thing you want to do is to let an old ornament go for a pittance and discover something similar on sale in an antique dealer's for ten times as much.

Car-boot sales and garage sales are excellent ways of getting rid of a range of goods of no particular individual value, items such as toys and Lego, paperbacks, old CDs and general household clutter. You need to be a bit organized, pricing goods beforehand and equipping yourself with bags and newspapers for wrapping glass and china. It also takes a degree of stamina – most events start early and take place in all weathers. Find out which sales are the best attended in your area, and accept only cash on the day.

Selling direct to shops is another option. Clothing with a designer label can be sold to second-hand shops specializing in upmarket clothing. Some of these will offer cash on the spot; others operate on a sale-or-return basis. Similarly, second-hand book dealers may price a collection for you, if you have more than a few books to get rid of. If you are selling furniture, look out for stores that sell designs of a similar period or type. Even furniture dating back only a decade or so counts as desirable 'retro' these days.

For items that are difficult to price and especially those that have greater intrinsic value, selling at auction is often the best option. You will have to pay commission on the sale, but you stand less chance of being deceived about a piece's true worth than if you were attempting to sell to a single dealer.

Finally, there is always eBay. You need to register to use the site and pay a fee for each listing and a percentage of each sale. Adding a digital photograph to your listing generally speeds up the sale. Old Conran furniture fetches a good price on eBay, I'm glad to say.

Throwing away

What you can't donate, recycle or sell will have to be thrown away. Ordinary waste can go out with the household rubbish; toxic chemicals, including old paint, engine oil and insecticides, need more careful disposal. Many local tips or dumps provide facilities for safe disposal of such items; consult your local council.

Take special care when throwing away documents that provide details of your name, address and banking arrangements. Identity theft is a fast-growing crime and all it takes is one or two pieces of paper with the relevant information and you could find yourself falling victim to it. For this reason, shredders have become one of the fastest-selling household items in recent years.

LEFT: It is not merely perishable foodstuffs and provisions that you keep in the refrigerator that have a shelf life. Basics of the store cupboard or larder, including condiments, herbs and spices, also deteriorate over time. While they may or may not go off, they will certainly lose their flavour.

ABOVE: These open-fronted box shelves offer an understated and ungimmicky way of storing collections of CDs and DVDs.

ASSESSMENT

No clearout or major overhaul is complete without taking the opportunity to assess the way in which you are storing those possessions you want to keep. Once you have disposed of everything that is surplus to requirements, for whatever reason, take a long hard look at what remains and where and how you are storing it.

In this context, the two principal factors that should guide your decisions are accessibility and frequency of use. In general, those items which you use daily should be stored or housed close at hand, in the immediate vicinity of where you will be using them. Possessions that are used rarely or seasonally can be stored more remotely and brought out only when you require them. There are, of course, exceptions to this basic rule. While it is to be hoped that the first-aid box will see only rare outings, when it is required, the need is urgent. Such emergency supplies should be kept in an accessible location where they are easy to retrieve quickly.

Clutter is not simply too much stuff; it is also stuff in the wrong place. This aspect of creative review allows you to keep in step with the changes that different life stages throw your way, which, in turn, entails thinking about how you actually use different areas in your home at the present time. Increasingly, for example, kitchens are not simply defined as places where food is prepared, but are taking on many of the same multipurpose roles as general living areas. If you regularly listen to music in the kitchen, it makes sense to provide a place to store CDs neatly rather than in scattered piles on the countertop. If the kitchen is the place where young children play under your watchful eye, allocating some storage space for toys and games will allow you to restore basic order quickly and effortlessly after they have gone to bed, without having to make endless trips up and down the stairs. Toys are not normally what one expects to find in a kitchen cupboard, but at this particular stage it is a far better use of available space than filling up the same cupboard with gadgets you use once in a blue moon.

Close at hand

Anything which you use daily should be kept close at hand, preferably in the area where it will be used. In many cases, this means out on view. When you put an item that is frequently used away in a cupboard or drawer, you add the task of retrieval into the equation. By the same token, anything that is close at hand should be in frequent use; if it's not, think about putting it elsewhere.

The kitchen is one area where you need to be able to reach for things instinctively without having to pause and consider where they might be. Utensils and provisions on daily call should be either visible – hanging from racks or on open shelves – or stored in the top drawer of units, or within cupboards near the main areas of activity. Items needed rarely but acutely, such as fuses, bulbs and first-aid boxes, also need a dedicated location that is readily accessible.

ABOVE: The way you organize your home should reflect the way you live and your priorities. For those who work out on a regular basis, it makes perfect sense to keep exercise equipment in the bedroom, particularly if there is plenty of floor space for physical movement.

Possessions to keep close at hand:

• Soaps, shampoos, toothbrushes, toothpaste and other essential items of personal care.

• Basic cooking provisions and utensils, such as wooden spoons, knives, cooking oils, salt and pepper, washing-up liquid. Tailor your selection to what you actually eat and how you like to cook. If you don't use a great deal of sugar, there is no reason to keep a sugar bowl on the kitchen counter.

• Bills and other paperwork requiring immediate attention. Keep these separate from other correspondence and in a location where they won't be forgotten.

• Homework and school projects.

• Outdoor-wear appropriate to the season.

• Remote controls for television, video and CD players, along with listing guides.

• Any possession that gives you particular delight should be out on view where you can appreciate it.

• Favourite toys or games. Children have their own preferences, and the most favoured toys are often taken to bed with them.

ABOVE LEFT: Basic cooking utensils that are in daily use – and a roll of paper towel for tackling accidental spills immediately – are among those items that need to be kept close at hand in the kitchen.

OPPOSITE: In any working area the tools for the job in hand need to be within easy reach on the desktop. Don't overclutter your desk, however, or you will start to lose the ability to think clearly and freely.

ABOVE: Jars of preserves and foodstuffs which you buy in bulk can be kept in a pantry cupboard a little out of the way of the main kitchen area. You won't need to replenish stocks every day.
OPPOSITE: Well-designed kitchen storage combines a run of closed base units with modular display shelving. Open shelves give a much lighter look than wall units.

At one remove

Many household provisions and belongings see occasional but unpredictable use. It is fair to say that the greater proportion of concealed storage, fitted or unfitted, will be given over to housing such items. It may be your best dishes or glasses which are brought out for special occasions; it may be a particular type of pan, such as a wok, that you don't use every day or every week, but certainly a few times a month; it may be books or reference material to which you intermittently refer.

Possessions that fall into this category generally merit being kept in the general location where they will be used, although at one remove from the main areas of activity. Any further afield and the difficulty of retrieval will reduce the number of times you will bother to use them. At the same time, it is worth keeping an eye on how often you do use them: if 'from time to time' becomes 'never', you should think about getting rid of them completely, or consigning them to deep storage.

Possessions to keep at one remove:

• Files and documents relating to your work in hand, rather than your career history.
• Special ingredients, condiments and provisions that are not required daily or weekly. These should be reviewed periodically to ensure they are not past their use-by date. (Many foods that are only a little past their sell-by date are perfectly safe to eat – exercise a little judgement; not shellfish and other highly perishable foods, obviously.)
• Cooking equipment and utensils with specialized functions.
• 'Best' sets of china, glassware or tableware.
• Bulk supplies of everyday items, and spare linen and bedding.

LEFT AND OPPOSITE: Underneath the arches … redundant railway arches serve a wide range of purposes these days, including storage and garaging. Before you rent storage space, make sure that what you are intending to store is valuable enough to warrant the payment of rental fees.

Deep storage

Belongings that should be kept in deep storage include those that are used yearly or seasonally, as well as documentation, records or sentimental items which either must be kept for legal purposes or which form your personal archive. You may also wish to put things away that you know you will need in a year or so. Never consign an article to deep storage as a way of avoiding making a decision whether or not it should be disposed of. Deep storage

that is serving as a graveyard for things you never use or don't like is just as much of a waste of space as any other cluttered area.

The best places for deep storage are attics, basements, garages, sheds and any other location that is out of the run of the household. 'Deepest' of all are long-term storage facilities away from the home. In all cases, making sure keeping conditions are adequate is paramount – when things are this far out of sight, they are well and truly out of mind, which means you may only discover damage when it is too late. You don't want to fill your basement with boxes

of documents, for example, only to find them spoiled by damp when you need to retrieve them. Cellars and basements may need humidifiers to keep excess moisture at bay. If you are storing heavy boxes in attics, you may need to strengthen the joists first, and you will certainly need to board out the area. Buildings such as garages and sheds, which are unheated, will be unsuitable for storing certain types of belongings that require a warm, dry atmosphere.

Label whatever items you put away and keep a list so that you know exactly what you have stored, and where. All containers

should be lidded and, if possible, made of a sturdier material than cardboard in order to withstand any damage of the type caused by a sudden leak, for example.

Certain categories of belongings may require specific keeping conditions. If you are storing clothes in deep storage, for example, they should be clean, packed in garment bags interleaved with acid-free tissue and kept at a stable level of humidity and temperature, with no exposure to sunlight. This will ensure that they remain in good condition until they are needed again.

Possessions to keep in deep storage:

• Christmas decorations and catering-sized pans, dishes and platters that are used once a year at most.

• Seasonal items of clothing.

• Seasonal items of sports equipment.

• Records such as tax returns and other documentation that must be kept for legal purposes.

• Toys and clothing that you are keeping until Child Number Two or Three comes along.

• Only keep valuable belongings in rented storage, otherwise you may find you are paying more to store your possessions than they are actually worth.

Storage ergonomics

In storage terms, the science of ergonomics formulates optimum heights and depths for shelves, worktops and cupboards by reference to basic human dimensions and movements. This has particular relevance for any hard-working area in the home, such as kitchens and workrooms, where there is the need to carry out a range of activities efficiently and safely.

• Reach is a critical factor when it comes to storing things that are in frequent use. Anything you use regularly should be kept between waist and eye level.

• High-level storage, which can only be accessed by a ladder or stool, should be reserved for lighter, less bulky items.

• Heavy things should be stored at waist level or just below so that there is less risk of back strain when retrieving them.

• If space is limited, consider eye-level cabinets rather than floor units. Bending down takes up more room than reaching up.

• Never fill boxes to the point where you can only move them with assistance. A greater number of smaller containers are more accessible for items in deep storage than a single trunk that weighs a ton and is impossible to shift.

ABOVE: Arrange books and other items on shelves so that those you refer to most frequently are in easy reach, which means between waist and eye level.

OPPOSITE: These kitchen shelves and compartments are slightly away from the main areas of activity, which maximizes space where it is needed.

2. Types of Storage

There are three main ways of organizing your belongings: in fitted or built-in storage, in storage furniture or containers, or out on view, a method that shades into display. Within each category, it is possible to express almost every decorative style, from a sleek contemporary look to a more rustic approach. In practice, while most homes will include storage of all three basic types, the balance between fitted and unfitted areas will vary, according to how much space you have at your disposal, as well as your individual preferences.

It could well be argued that how and where you keep your possessions defines the appearance of your home to a far greater extent than any other element. Wherever possible you should take the opportunity to plan storage early on in the design process. Whether you go the fitted or unfitted route, this will result in a more considered result than if you react retrospectively and add some shelves here, or a few more containers there, once your belongings have started to accumulate.

OPPOSITE: How you choose to organize your belongings – whether out on display or behind closed doors – will inevitably define the overall appearance of your home, as well as the way in which it functions.

MAKING THE MOST OF SPACE

Before you begin to put storage systems into place, it is well worth taking a look at your home as a whole to determine whether you are making the best use of available space. Unless every nook and cranny is already stuffed to the gills, you may find you have more space than you think in areas with storage potential you might otherwise have overlooked. Many storage problems simply arise from bad habits, and a thorough spatial review can help you to take the blinkers off and see your home in a new light.

Thinking about the whole picture, rather than approaching the issue on a piecemeal basis, can have a dramatic knock-on effect, freeing whole areas of clutter and possibly allowing an entire room to be put to a new and welcome use. It's rather like doing a jigsaw puzzle in three dimensions. Perhaps, for example, you have an attic which has become the repository for a few odd boxes, but which is otherwise under-used for storage, as well as a box room or storage closet that is filled to bursting point. You might consider converting the attic into a fully fledged room to serve as an additional bedroom or workspace, and thus relieve pressure on the rest of your home – a strategy that will also add to its value. Equally effective, but much cheaper and less disruptive, would be to lay a serviceable floor if there isn't one already, invest in a secure loft ladder and fit out the attic as a dedicated storage space for clutter that is otherwise silting up in other areas. Suddenly that box room that you could barely enter is empty and could well serve as a separate dressing room, in which case your bedroom, minus your wardrobe, will become a much more serene place. Not everyone has a box room,

attic, basement or garage, but most homes have hidden corners or under-used areas that can be exploited in a similar fashion.

The circulation space of landings, hallways and stairs can be particularly useful for storage. Properly executed in a wholehearted manner, built-in storage can lend welcome architectural character to such spaces. In older properties, circulation areas tend to be on the generous side. If a hallway is wide enough, consider putting up shelves floor to ceiling to house a library, or build seamless cupboards along one wall to take outdoor wear, files for your home office or any other paraphernalia. A landing might be large enough for an armoire where you can store linen without compromising basic traffic routes, while wide stairways can usefully accommodate shelving. If the ceiling height is sufficient, back hallways can provide space overhead for racking bicycles and similar bulky items.

The staggered space below the staircase is often used as an ad hoc storage area in many homes. Rather than treat it as a dumping ground for items that really should be in deep storage or discarded altogether, take the opportunity to equip it as a proper

ABOVE: Making use of redundant areas, such as the staggered space below the stairs, is much easier if you have the opportunity to redesign an area from scratch. Here, pull-out shelves have been neatly integrated under the stairs, preserving the sleek, pristine look of the uncluttered kitchen.

storage area where things can be readily retrieved and where they can be maintained in good condition. Freestanding shelf units or containers of staggered heights constitute an 'unfitted' approach; built-in shelving, cupboards, drawers or cubbyholes provide a fitted solution. If the stairway is open rather than enclosed, you can also use the area underneath to store outdoor clothes, hanging from a neat array of hooks, or house smaller items in a chest of drawers.

Considering circulation areas as potential sites for storage also gives you with the opportunity to review basic traffic routes around your home. If there is a choice of entrances to a given area, for example, it is likely that one will be favoured over the other. In that

case, it is an option to fill in one doorway and win more wall area both in the hall and within the room itself, space that can be used to extend a run of kitchen units, for example, or for additional shelving.

Looking at the big picture can also lead you to reassess the basic allocation of rooms, which may have an equal impact on the way your home functions as a whole. When children are very young, their play is largely floor-based. If you give them the largest bedroom while they are still of an age to share, toys are less likely to overrun the rest of the household. Or you may find that you are maintaining a separate dining room for the sake of appearances, but rarely eat there. Any area that is seeing such infrequent use is ripe for takeover.

OPPOSITE LEFT: Halls and landings can often usefully decant clutter from living areas. Here, the connecting area immediately adjacent to the main bedroom has been fitted out for clothes storage, with hanging space, cubbyholes and drawers.

OPPOSITE RIGHT: This flight of stairs, custom-designed and constructed, incorporates drawers slotted in at the back of the treads.

ABOVE LEFT: An ingenious variation on understairs storage is provided by this arrangement where books and magazines are neatly slotted in under the broad wooden stair treads – handy for retrieval, too.

ABOVE RIGHT: A custom-designed stair-cum-store cupboard features stepped cabinets faced in a warm wood. The tops of these cupboards serve as half of the stair treads, while the remaining treads are in the form of lift-up flaps.

OPPOSITE: Double-height spaces offer great potential for committed storage solutions, such as this wall of shelving, accessed both from the ladder and from the mezzanine level above.

RIGHT: A library stair with a difference, this custom-designed staircase incorporates open shelving underneath for books.

BELOW RIGHT: A less expensive solution for a standard or existing staircase is simply to enclose the area under the stairs by adding cupboard doors. The examples shown here are made in tongue-and-groove panelling.

FITTED STORAGE

Built-in storage embraces a variety of what one might call architectural storage solutions, from off-the-peg kitchen and bathroom units to custom-designed and made cupboards and shelving. This approach has an obvious application where there are fixed points in a layout, such as the servicing arrangements in a kitchen or bathroom. Fitted storage is a supremely workable way of integrating what might otherwise be disparate fixtures, provided you can still access the servicing.

Although built-in storage necessarily involves the sacrifice of a certain amount of floor area, it is often the best approach when it comes to small rooms or multipurpose areas where a range of unfitted solutions, such as traditional freestanding storage furniture or containers of some sort, would be visually obtrusive. In aesthetic terms, fitted storage goes hand in hand with the clean lines of contemporary spaces. No minimalist could be without a seamless wall of cupboards to conceal the mundanity of everyday objects and possessions, while built-in cupboards formed part of what Le Corbusier, the founder of Modernism, called 'interior equipment'. At its most self-effacing, fitted storage reads as a wall that is barely interrupted by the flush panels of door fronts, which are openable by either concealed chamfered finger grips or press catches. Such installations require precise planning and expert construction if they are both to look good and to function properly: any doors and drawers must operate smoothly and fit perfectly. This is even more the case where there is a degree of articulation – for example, panels or flaps that slide out or swing round should do so without requiring you to put in a vast degree of effort.

While fitted storage is often bracketed with modern design, it does not necessarily have to equal minimalism. Many fitted systems contribute more positively to overall décor in terms of colour, material and finish. Glossy red kitchen cabinets, for example, can contribute an emphatic splash of colour and glamour in an otherwise understated functional space.

Much inspiration can be gained by studying tightly fitted spaces such as caravans and boats, places where every square inch has to work. What makes such places intrinsically appealing is that they are completely operable – tables pull out, beds fold down and lockers tucked into every nook and cranny provide room for stowing away essentials. Similarly, commercial and industrial systems are often supremely functional and can be a fruitful source of ideas for storage at home, even if you do not particularly want to import the 'no frills' aesthetic.

OPPOSITE: A sweeping, curved storage wall, dividing a kitchen/living area from the bedrooms, incorporates kitchen cupboards at the far end with open shelving modules for books; on the other side is a place to display children's artwork. This type of architectural approach is both practical and spatially dynamic.

ABOVE: There are many ingenious built-in systems available on the market to help you make the most of your kitchen space. These pull-out shelves are a good solution in a narrow area and can be accessed from either side. Here, the shelves are used to store glassware, but similar units can also be used as larder cupboards.

Planning fitted storage

A good starting point when it comes to planning built-in storage is to make a basic sketch plan of the area in question, whether it is a whole room, an alcove or a wall where you intend to put up shelving. If your storage needs are more extensive, you may wish to map out most of your home so that you can look at different types of solution.

The first step is to take detailed measurements. It is important to be as accurate as possible right from the outset. Fitted storage is particularly intolerant of mistakes, and any anomalies will be all too glaring once the cupboard is built or the shelves have gone up. Use a proper steel measure. If you are not confident about measuring, get a friend to help you.

The next step is to use the measurements you have taken to draw up a plan. Use graph paper and work to a reasonable scale so that you can properly assess the impact of what you are proposing. Mark onto the plan any existing features in the room or area that you do not intend to change. These might include servicing points, power sockets and switches, architectural details and other built-in elements.

Once you have completed the plan you can try out different storage solutions. It can be useful to refer to catalogues to gain an appreciation of the common height and depth of fitted units or wardrobes so that you don't go ahead and commission storage which is either too cramped or too roomy for what you intend to put into it. It can be useful to draw up the shapes of fitted elements separately, using the same scale, and cut them out so that they can be moved about on your drawing to test out suitable locations. Bear in mind that you will need as much room again in front of drawers so that they can be pulled out and their contents freely accessed. Similarly, cupboard doors require clearance, unless they are sliding, and there should be adequate space in front of shelves so that you can easily bend down and retrieve items from the lowest.

Needless to say, it is also important to factor in to the equation the quantity and dimensions of whatever it is that you are intending to store. When in doubt, measure the item or items in question, and add in a generous margin for future acquisitions.

ABOVE LEFT: Built-in storage cubicles provide a useful means of organizing different types of belongings – and a convenient and not overly prominent place for the television.

ABOVE: Giving over an entire wall to storage looks neat and well considered. This arrangement features a combination of vertical cubbyholes, overhead lockers and closet space with open shelving.

LEFT: Similar to library systems, these fitted storage units have shelving on both sides to make the most of available space. Each unit can be rotated to provide access to the contents.

ABOVE: Shelving is the ideal storage solution for many different types of belongings, not merely books. These robust shelves house a significant collection while contributing a considerable degree of character to the room. If you have many books, you will need to adopt some form of basic organization – by author or subject, for example – in order to put your hands on the book you want without too much difficulty.

OPPOSITE: Double-height spaces allow you to extend storage vertically, although do bear in mind that you will need a secure ladder to fetch items from the uppermost shelves or cubbyholes.

Designing fitted storage

In general terms, built-in storage looks best if it is designed to complement the existing architectural character of the space. This does not necessarily mean that you have to replicate every last detail. In a period room, for example, crisp modern fittings can make a highly effective contrast that in no way detracts from or undermines existing features. In fact, such a bold insertion is invariably much more successful than a half-hearted attempt to copy period style with applied trim.

What is more important than extraneous details or mouldings is basic proportion and scale. Here, it is a question of working with the layout so that you achieve a considered approach – shelving an entire wall, for example, not a portion of it, or treating both alcoves on each side of a chimney breast in the same way. In older properties, a visually comfortable break is about one-third of the way up the wall, a height that conforms to the position of a dado rail. You can use this position to mark a shift between fitted or closed cupboards below and open shelving above.

In modern homes, architectural detail may well be fairly minimal. Flush doors and panels and simple shelving in steel, glass or wood strike an appropriate contemporary note. Extending cupboard doors floor to ceiling helps fitted storage to read as part of the wall, rather than an obtrusive addition. A horizontal emphasis can also be highly effective. Low-level shelving that runs around the perimeter of the room can add a different dynamic to a space.

Another part of the design equation is thinking about materials and finishes. Where concealment is required, any material that can be painted or finished to resemble the walls is ideal. MDF (medium density fibreboard), the mainstay of television makeover programmes, is a popular material for fitted storage because it is strong and dimensionally stable, and it is easy to paint. Semi-transparent fronts, doors or drawers, made of glass, Perspex (Plexiglas) or plastic, help to keep the effect light and spacious, especially if the panels are backlit. Fabric screens and blinds can work well in bedrooms or other areas where a softer, more upholstered approach is required.

There are, however, occasions when it might be appropriate for fitted storage to take centre stage. When everything else in

ABOVE: Floor-level lighting under the built-in clothes closets, as well as the bed, provides a visual lift. The interiors of the closets contain drawers and hanging space.

RIGHT: Sliding floor-to-ceiling panels conceal recessed shelving and can be moved across for access. Shelving tends to look more considered when it does not stop short of the ceiling.

ABOVE LEFT AND RIGHT: In eighteenth-century interiors, decorating or shelving one side of a door so that it blended in with the walls was a common way of creating visual unity within a room. This contemporary version of the 'jib door', as such features are traditionally termed, treats the door as a simple opening panel within the fitted kitchen.

an area is simple and reticent, a bold texture, colour or finish can inject a welcome degree of vitality. Kitchen units veneered in a dark wood, for example, or brightly coloured shiny metal bathroom cabinets, marry style with storage to great effect. Bear in mind that the basic carcass of built-in storage can be constructed in a relatively cheap material, which will leave more in your budget for doors, panels and drawer fronts.

Building fitted storage

Unless you are a dab hand at carpentry or do-it-yourself, you will almost certainly require professional help to achieve a successful result. There are several routes open to you.

The first option is to sketch out what you want and hire someone to build it for you. If a project is small in scale, this hands-on approach may well be cost-effective, and there is the added bonus that you will also be able to specify precisely which finishes, detailing and materials you require. You do need to be satisfied that whoever you hire to carry out the work has done similar jobs before, and to an acceptable standard. It is also essential that you plan very carefully so that the end result actually works properly – for example, that shelving is accessible, doors open the right way and cupboards are the right height.

The second option is to opt for one of the many fitted storage systems available on the market. These range from units specifically designed for kitchens and bathrooms, to fitted wardrobes, shelving systems and other general-purpose built-in solutions. Many large retailers or suppliers have in-house design services to help you come up with a result that suits your needs and the space at your disposal, which can be a particular advantage when planning fitted rooms such as kitchens and bathrooms. Similarly, most of these suppliers provide their own fitting service and many even offer financial packages, which enables you to spread the cost over time. At the upper end of the market, some companies will adapt a fitted system to your specific requirements, which enables you to come close to a fully bespoke result.

The third approach is to engage the services of a designer or an architect. If you are faced with many related storage and spatial issues, or are thinking of completely redoing an entire area of your home – for example, the kitchen – expert design help can be invaluable. Designers and architects are skilled at coming up with spatial solutions and may be able to devise a scheme that improves the way your home works overall and not merely in the area in question. Unlike major retailers or mass-market outlets, they don't have product ranges to sell and may be able to save you money while furnishing you with a more original result both in terms of design and materials.

Fitted interiors

To be efficient and workable, fitted storage must be tailored in some fashion to its contents. Without a degree of customization, the basic module of the kitchen unit, for example, is simply blank space that does not accommodate in any sense the disparate shapes and sizes of kitchen equipment and provisions. Movable shelves, inset racks and pull-out trays can help to provide a more specific context for different storage requirements.

The same is true of bespoke fitted cupboards. In terms of shelf depth and height, or the dimensions of cubbyholes or closets, the interior specification of cupboards should conform to what you intend to put in them or be subdivided in some way by appropriate containers so that you use the storage space to its full capacity. For example, if you line up shoes at the bottom of a cubbyhole measuring 60cm (2ft) square, you are wasting the greater proportion of the space available.

'Tidies' and organizers which can look a little uptight out on view come into their own when it comes to customizing cupboard interiors. Fabric pouches for shoes can be hung on the reverse of a closet door, for example, or open boxes can be used to segregate small items within a larger drawer.

Another important aspect to consider when it comes to the efficient functioning of fitted storage systems is the ease of retrieval of the items inside. Working walls of cupboards can house a great deal of disparate possessions – everything from entire wardrobes to personal paperwork, books and music collections. But the more extensive and discreet the storage system, the greater the risk that you will not be able to remember exactly where you have put everything. Opening drawer after drawer or cupboard after cupboard in order to find an essential document or piece of equipment will rapidly undermine efficiency. A sketch plan or

ABOVE LEFT: When it comes to designing fitted storage spaces, there is next to no margin for error if everything is not only to function as it should, but also to look seamless.

LEFT: Drawers fitted into a low-level ledge or plinth are unobtrusive and provide convenient places to store a variety of items from shoes to spare bedding or sweaters.

ABOVE AND RIGHT If you adopt this type of thorough-going approach to storage, and keep everything hidden away, you will really need some idea of what has been put where or you will waste a great deal of time opening one drawer after another. A diagram can be a useful way of jogging your memory.

LEFT: Drawers with blackboard fronts provide an easy means of identifying their contents. You can chalk up what each contains and, if you move things round at a future date, you can simply wipe clean the blackboard and relabel.

inventory can be an invaluable aid if you tend to forget whether the CDs are in the third cupboard from the right or the fourth.

Commodious fitted storage will need to be well lit so that you can see what is in the furthermost recesses. Information lights that are triggered by the opening of a door and that are switched off again automatically when the door is closed are useful in this respect. In the case of a walk-in closet, larder or similar storage room, however, an information light is unlikely to be adequate, and a proper switched light fitting will be required.

ABOVE: Tailor-made storage for a man's wardrobe includes a rack for ties, shallow drawers for shirts and shelving at high level for sweaters.
LEFT: Customizing the interiors of kitchen units allows you to house a diverse range of equipment and accessories while preserving a neat, uncluttered appearance.

UNFITTED STORAGE

Unfitted storage encompasses everything from traditional pieces of storage furniture, such as chests, chests of drawers, wardrobes and armoires, to hanging rails, pegboards and simple boxes, baskets and other types of container. Many people find this approach innately appealing – there is something about containers, in particular, that seems to enshrine the notion of possession. For those who do not expect to be in their present home very long, unfitted storage can represent a sensible investment, as pieces can be packed up and moved with the rest of the furniture.

Another advantage of this way of organizing your home is that it is relatively direct and uncomplicated: you buy a container and put things in it. There is no waiting around for the carpenter to show up and build you a cupboard, for example. However, that same directness can pose a problem. If you respond to all your storage needs in this ad hoc way, you may quickly find yourself sharing your home with a collection of disparate containers and pieces of furniture that do not sit very well together. As with any other aspect of storage, planning goes a long way to achieving a successful and practical result.

It is also fair to say that unfitted storage tends to take up more floor space than the sleeker fitted variety. Larger pieces of freestanding storage furniture may have capacious interiors, but they also have a dominating effect on the rest of the room and require plenty of breathing space if they are not to be overwhelming, either visually or physically. Too many such pieces in a given area and you might begin to find it awkward to move about from place to place.

Unfitted storage furniture has something of a traditional image, but there are many contemporary options available from which to choose. Some of these are migrants from commercial or retail sectors, and others are reinterpretations of standard pieces in a more modern design idiom.

Storage furniture

For long periods of history, the principal item of storage furniture was the chest, a simple and relatively portable means of storing what few possessions most people owned. Storage furniture only began to become more elaborate with the growth of the middle classes in the late seventeenth to eighteenth centuries, and the

OPPOSITE: Freestanding storage furniture ranges from traditional designs such as chests, dressers (hutches) and armoires to salvaged pieces that might once have been used in commercial or retail applications.

increase in the numbers and types of belongings that they began to accumulate. From this period date such types of furniture as the dressing table, with its drawers for the accoutrements of personal style, as well as the secretaire, which combined a writing slope with pigeonholes, drawers and a closed cabinet for books. Chests of drawers took on the all-purpose role of chests for organizing and storing clothing and other types of linen.

Many early pieces of storage furniture were as ingenious as they were beautiful, serving a number of different functions. Others were very specific: the canterbury, for example, which first appeared at the end of the eighteenth century, was originally designed as a means of storing sheet music.

When it comes to choosing storage furniture today, you should first and foremost be guided by basic practicality. A chest of drawers, for instance, is just as useful for keeping folded linen and clothing as it was hundreds of years ago. At a time when letter writing has largely been supplanted by email and the computer keyboard has taken the place of the writing pen, however, period-style desks and other types of writing furniture may present you with a functional mismatch. That is one reason why I find it so regrettable that many people persist in concealing modern equipment such as televisions and hi-fi systems within reproduction pieces of furniture that were originally devised to serve quite a different purpose.

Storage furniture which continues to earn its keep includes the ever-popular kitchen dresser (hutch), the cosy centrepiece (along with an Aga, of course) of many country kitchens, and quite a few in towns as well. Other pieces, such as the bookcase and the sideboard, have shed their former monumentality in favour of crisp lines and simple detailing. The sideboard seems a particularly quaint item at a time when fewer people have separate dining rooms; reinvented as a long horizontal cabinet, however, it serves many different storage purposes within multipurpose spaces.

Storage furniture recycled from non-domestic contexts can also add a touch of wit and originality to the interior. Reclaimed shop fittings, school lockers and retail display fittings have been popular for sufficiently long to command quite high prices these days. One or two such pieces are generally enough for any given area unless that area is really very large.

TOP: There are many contemporary designs of freestanding storage furniture on the market, some of which are also mobile. These units roll out on castors to provide access from both sides.
ABOVE: A long, low wooden unit, combining open and concealed storage, provides a spatial divider alongside a staircase.

OPPOSITE: Reclaimed wooden lockers provide extensive storage for a wide variety of possessions. Here a hi-fi system has been fitted into one locker on the top row, with speakers on each side.

Addressing the need for space-saving, there are a number of different beds on the market that incorporate storage below the frame. In some designs, long drawers are fitted so that the whole area beneath the bed can be used to house linen, bulky jumpers and similar articles. In others, the bed hinges up to reveal storage compartments below. Such pieces recall the classic Shaker sewing chair, fitted with a drawer under the seat to store sewing supplies.

Storage units

Relatively anonymous, storage units provide freestanding storage for a wide variety of possessions, as well as a means of display. Many units are available as part of modular systems that can be extended or configured in different ways. Some come in the form of cubes that can be stacked into a tower or combined into working walls. Others have optional castors, doors and shelves so that you can customize them to your specification.

A key factor is robustness. Cheap, flimsy units will not take the weight of books or CDs, and may present a hazard as they can be readily tipped over without wall anchorage. Stout commercial designs in steel or steel wire have greater stability and are often handsome enough to be used in living areas as well as behind the scenes.

Judicious placing of a storage unit can serve to separate different activities within an open-plan space. In the case of open shelf units or modules, light and views will be only minimally screened.

Trolleys and mobile units add flexibility to storage arrangements and are particularly useful in fitted rooms such as kitchens and bathrooms, where you may require items to be on hand for limited periods. Some designs for kitchen use incorporate chopping blocks on top, effectively providing additional counter space.

As well as all-purpose storage units, there are many designs that are more specific in their intended use. CD towers and racks designed around the dimensions of the CD case are a good example. If you have a CD collection that threatens to keep expanding, choose a type of unit that looks attractive in multiples, rather than a number of different units that add to visual clutter, or adopt a different method of storage entirely, such as on shelves or in drawers.

ABOVE: Utensils, pans and other items of kitchen equipment in constant use look good hanging from a rail above the main preparation area. Make sure what you display in this fashion does see regular use or you may well find yourself having to clean items more often than you would otherwise need to.

OPPOSITE: Hanging rails satisfy a child's need to see some of their favourite things on display – and a parent's need to impose a little order and organization.

Rails, racks, hooks and pegboards

One of the key ways of enhancing space is to keep the floor free from clutter. Rails, racks, hooks and pegboards allow you to exploit wall space and hang up possessions in an orderly way. This is a particularly good solution for hallways, utility areas and workshops where retrieving what you need is made easier by having it out on view. Such out-of-the-way locations also address the principal disadvantage of this method of storage, which is that it tends to look rather busy.

Almost anything from garden tools to bicycles can be racked or hung up, provided the means of suspension is robust and securely plugged into the wall. Do-it-yourself outlets are a good source of basic racking systems for sheds and other utility areas. For areas of the home that are more open to view, there is a huge range of more stylish options from which to choose, from sleek contemporary brushed-steel hooks to wooden pegboards.

The Shakers were famously keen on hanging things from the wall; in their case, from wooden pegboards that ran around the perimeter of the room at cornice level. While they used pegboards to hang up chairs, brooms, brushes – in fact, anything not in use at the time – in most homes, pegboards are the means for hanging up towels and outdoor wear, or of organizing a particular category of possession, such as ties or belts, on the backs of closet doors. In family bathrooms and children's rooms think about providing hooks or a pegboard at a lower level to make it easy for them to access.

The kitchen is one of the few areas in the home where racks and hanging rails add more positively to the visual appeal of the space. Suspended from a rail near the worksurface, gleaming pans and utensils, along with other articles that form part of the batterie de cuisine, combine basic practicality with an almost sculptural display.

The same is not true of clothes rails, which migrated from the retail sector some years ago to become one of the most popular means of clothes storage. Unless your bedroom is large, clothes rails can be very intrusive. At the same time, they expose clothing to dust and fading from light, which means they are best used to store only a capsule wardrobe, with the rest of your clothing in more protected surroundings.

Magazine and newspaper racks, like CD towers, address a particular storage issue. A neat pile of magazines on a table has never bothered me, but if you are the sort of person who likes to rack their reading matter, there are a wide range of designs on the market, from wall-mounted metal racks to V- or W-shaped racks that sit on the floor. At least when the rack is overflowing, you know that it's time to sort through the back issues.

Containers

Many types of storage take the form of a container – a drawer is essentially a container, so is a safe, and so is the bowl where you keep your spare change. In all their various guises, from cardboard boxes to glass bottles to log baskets, containers are one of the principal building blocks of home organization. More than that, they appeal to our basic instinct to squirrel things away in homes of their own, which is at least part of the pleasure of owning things.

Putting things in containers is a way of keeping them both secure and segregated. A key aspect to consider is one of scale. In general, small items should go in smaller containers or in containers within containers – for example, the small plastic box where you keep the spare fuses inside the kitchen drawer. Bigger items or foodstuffs which you use in greater quantities need to be kept in larger containers. There is, however, a limit to how large the container can be and still be practical. A huge basket is not a very sensible solution to the problem of toy storage – it will simply get tipped out all over the floor as your children hunt for the single toy they want to play with that morning. Similarly, filling a trunk to the brim with heavy objects means that it will be impossible to lift.

Containers are ideal for keeping like with like – nails or screws, for example, or multipiece games and puzzles. What they should never be used for is catch-alls for unrelated items – that is simply a case of ignoring your mess, rather than getting to grips with it.

By and large containers represent one of the cheapest ways of organizing your home. Inexpensive boxes in cardboard, metal, canvas or plastic, box files and raffia baskets can all be pressed into service to declutter everything from the home office to the children's room. Otherwise, you can always recycle containers – soaking the labels off jam (jelly) jars, covering shoeboxes in wrapping paper or hanging onto pastille tins for storing small items such as buttons. Lids are a good idea if there is a risk that the container might be accidentally spilled, especially if you are storing things on a long-term basis. Clear containers allow you to read their contents at a glance; coloured containers signal whose is whose. Otherwise, you may need to label the outside in some way. If the containers are going to be out on view, they should be the same basic type or style. Food storage jars come in families of different sizes to suit the type of ingredient you are storing.

If you have to keep valuable items in the home, don't store them in locked boxes. Any box with a lock tells a thief that the contents are valuable. Instead, invest in a home safe that is designed to be concealed in the floor or wall, or think about renting a safe deposit box at the bank. Some chests and desks have secret drawers.

I appreciate fine things, but I don't keep anything really valuable at home for the simple reason that I could not bear to live with the type of security that would be required. I have simple, unobtrusive security and always lock doors and windows. When you need to install expensive alarm systems, and put bars on the windows and doors, your entire home becomes a container and you are the one locked in it. It's no way to live.

OPPOSITE: A wooden bench includes storage space in the box of the seat. Shaker furniture often displays this type of charming practicality.

RIGHT: Containers – trunks, baskets, hat boxes, old luggage – exert a powerful appeal. They are the least expensive and most immediate storage solution.

DISPLAY

In every room in the home, any possessions that you choose to keep out on view – on open shelving, hung on the wall or from a rail, on a table or mantelpiece – should either be contributing to your enjoyment of your home or be in daily or constant use. If preferable, they can do both.

One of the easiest ways to put a fresh face on your home is to change the items you keep on display. Strangely, however, these particular possessions are the ones that rarely seem to move from the spot where you first placed them.

When you are having a major overhaul or spring clean, or when a room is being redecorated, take the opportunity to rethink what you put on display. If the same picture has been hanging in the same spot over the fireplace for years, the chances are you won't really be appreciating it any more. Familiarity, in this case, breeds not so much contempt as invisibility. Changing your displays, on the other hand, brings a frisson of delight back into your experience of the space – providing something new to snag the attention as you pass by the window on the landing or gaze up from your desk at the shelves on the wall. Pack away the pictures or objects that have become stale with overexposure and place them in deep storage – or, better still, sell them or give them away to allow room in your life for a new acquisition.

We are all collectors to a greater or lesser degree, but those people who have become besotted by a specific type of object have a particular problem when it comes to storage and display. I used to collect butterflies and moths when I was a boy; today, what I most enjoying collecting is glass. I do like to use what I collect, however, rather than have it sitting around in display cases. The exception are the nineteen Bugatti pedal cars

ABOVE: My collection of Bugatti pedal cars hangs on the wall of the entrance hall in my house in the country. They somehow remind me of my first collecting passion – moths. **OPPOSITE:** Shelving that is cantilevered from the wall enhances decorative displays – there is little to interrupt what is placed on view.

that I acquired from a French collector and which now hang together on the wall of the entrance hall in my house in the country. Oddly enough, they remind me somewhat of beautiful moths, my first collecting passion.

One of my friends, Alistair McAlpine, is a renowned collector, so much so that he writes a regular column on the subject for the *World of Interiors* magazine. Over the years he has collected a diverse range of objects, from political buttons to ties to contemporary sculpture. It's the hunting down of each item that he particularly enjoys; once a collection is complete or the chase has lost its thrill, he sells or donates the collections.

If you find collecting irresistible you are going to have to adopt a similar strategy sooner or later to avoid being overrun by your ever-expanding collections. In this context, it is useful to bear in mind than many museums show only a fraction of what they hold. In some cases, it costs more to conserve the collection that the public never get a chance to see than to run the institution itself. If your home is in danger of turning into a museum, it inevitably will not be serving other functions very well.

By the same token, display only what you are prepared to look after. Items that are left out on view need regular dusting. If you don't want to devote a great proportion of your time to this type of basic household maintenance, cut down on the number of things you put on display. In addition, make sure that keeping objects on view will not damage them. For this reason, protect prints and drawings from direct natural light.

Display areas

Certain areas have always been favoured for display. In most homes, the mantelpiece has acquired totemic significance as a place for blatant one-upmanship – why else do invitations to important events from Very Important People often take up residence there? If not heavily embossed oblongs of white card, then there might be a particularly precocious example of an offspring's artwork or a souvenir from an exotic (and expensive) holiday. The mantelshelf is a natural display area because it sits at eye level right above the main focal point of the most public area in the house.

Other popular places for display include desktops – something to gaze upon in moments of boredom or when the muse deserts you – shelves and alcoves in living and dining areas and the tops of chests of drawers in bedrooms. Some places, however, become displays by default. The kitchen windowsill is a prime example of this. Chances are that very little of what is on 'display' in such locations really merits the attention. Often what is out on view is simply there to act as a visual trigger to tackle some piece of unfinished business. The button sitting on the shelf beside your collection of Clarice Cliff pots is there to nag you to sew it back on your shirt before it gets lost. Too many such items silting up in these locations and display areas become places your eye naturally tries to avoid because so much guilt is attached to them.

A large proportion of what people keep on display in their homes hangs on the wall – in the case of the typical teenager's bedroom,

every wall might be riotously collaged. Pictures and photographs give a home personality, colour and vitality, but, if they are dotted about from place to place, there is risk of visual overload. It is always more effective to designate one particular wall for display and to group pictures in a collection or to display a single painting prominently, with the remaining walls left clear to give some breathing space. If you are displaying a number of pictures of a similar type – all prints or all photographs of the same size, for example – it looks much more considered if they are framed the same way and hung in orderly rows. A more disparate collection requires a little experimentation to achieve a sympathetic arrangement. One strategy is to lay out all the pictures on the floor and play around with the order until you discover what looks comfortable. Often the larger pictures work best in the centre of the group, where they naturally draw the eye, with smaller ones around the periphery.

Hallways and other circulation areas are often good places for displaying pictures. For a start, they tend to be fairly anonymous spaces in need of some injection of vitality, and secondly they are also places of transition that we pass through only momentarily. Pictures hung here are less likely to lose their appeal than those in more prominent view.

The same strategy of grouping also applies to decorative objects – scattered over every surface they are distracting; clustered together they gain impact by association. If the objects are quirky, this also brings wit and amusement into play. Interleaving decorative objects in working walls otherwise devoted to books can help to lighten what might otherwise be rather enclosing.

If you have a special area for display, it is a good idea to take the trouble to light it properly, in order to reveal detail and accentuate material quality. Glass looks especially wonderful displayed in areas where it is lit by natural light or on glass shelving that emphasizes

ABOVE LEFT: Displays of everyday objects such as china are an easy and effective way of introducing colour and pattern into the interior. These vintage plates and cups add a homey touch.

LEFT: Objects can be displayed together successfully, even if their patterns are quite different. Because many of these bowls and cups feature the same colours, the effect is harmonious overall.

RIGHT: Photographs, prints and paintings, especially those that are relatively small in scale, work well hung in a group. You can work out the arrangement on the floor first to see what works best.

ABOVE: Crockery in a glass-fronted china cabinet makes a hospitable display in a dining area. Many traditional pieces of storage furniture, such as kitchen dressers (hutches), command high prices these days.
OPPOSITE: A vintage cupboard with its well-worn finish makes an evocative contrast to spare and robust concrete shelves and worktop.

its delicate transparency. Overtly textured objects often benefit from side-lighting – light trained across a surface naturally enhances its tactile quality by casting shadows in dips and hollows.

Accent lighting should not be overbright – of sufficient level to pick out a display in a focus of attention, but not so bright that the effect is overly theatrical. Discreet low-voltage halogen spots are good for highlighting single objects, while architectural strip lights concealed behind baffles can be used to illuminate display shelving in a soft even glow. Pictures need careful lighting – a spot will not do the trick if the picture is large, as it will simply cast light on a portion of it. There are a number of specialist picture lights on the market, many of which can be angled or adjusted so that the entire picture plane is evenly lit.

Working displays

The kitchen is a natural area for working displays. I always think that a kitchen where everything is hidden behind closed doors is a rather soulless place. As the kitchen is arguably the most nurturing place in the home, it is far more sympathetic to give at least some indication of what goes on there, whether the display is simply a bowl of beautiful fruit, an array of neat storage jars or a hanging rack of utensils. Practical objects, designed for a specific function and shaped to fit the hand, are attractive objects in their own right. If you keep on view those that you use on a regular basis, you are naturally increasing the efficiency with which you perform routine tasks, as well as providing something intriguing to look at.

Frequency of use, however, is the key. Whatever you use often will be washed regularly, and the dust and grease that can accumulate in even the best-ventilated kitchens will not have the opportunity to build up.

The kitchen dresser (hutch) is a traditional place of display, with its open shelves and plate racks serving as a home for a cheerful array of crockery, mugs and jugs. Again, bear in mind that if you do not make use of such items on a regular basis, you are giving yourself more housework to do, as they will need to be taken down and washed from time to time.

AREA-BY-AREA SOLUTIONS

3. Living Spaces

While the boundaries are increasingly coming down between private and public zones in the home, living areas retain much of their former status as hospitable social centres, where friends and visitors are welcomed and entertained. As such, there is still the expectation that a living area should be furnished and decorated so that it is not only comfortable, but also worthy of scrutiny. In many households, however, particularly where space is tight, living areas can become default zones, mopping up activities that cannot be accommodated elsewhere, along with all the attendant clutter. Perhaps your living room serves as a dining area, too; it may be where your home office is located. Good spatial planning and a sensitive approach to storage is necessary if a living area is to remain a pleasant place to relax, either privately or in company.

OPPOSITE: Storage should be as unobtrusive as possible in living areas so that the room's essential purpose, as a place for relaxation, can come to the fore. Here, low-level storage space has been built in under each window.

ASSESSING YOUR NEEDS

One way of gaining an insight into storage shortfalls in the living area is to go into the room and imagine that friends are coming over in half an hour. Is the area in basic order? If not, what type of things would you rush around tidying up or removing from the area altogether?

- Do you have to remove clutter before people can even sit down on the sofa or in chairs?
- Is there clear space on side tables or coffee tables?
- Are there used cups, plates or glasses lying around?
- Are there possessions in the living area which should really be housed elsewhere in the home – for example, articles of clothing, shoes or toys?
- Is there evidence of chores waiting to be tackled – for example, unanswered letters and bills?
- Is anything being stored temporarily on the floor, causing an obstruction to the way you move about the space?
- Are there DVDs, videos and CDs lying around out of their boxes?
- Are cables from media equipment snaking all over the place?
- Are there corners of the living area that you have not been able to clean thoroughly because too much clutter is in the way and it has become too mammoth a task to move it?
- Does the room look like a place where it is easy to relax? Does it feel light and airy, or are the walls closing in?
- What is the best feature of the room? Can it be properly appreciated, or is clutter confusing the picture?
- Do you use all of the furniture that is in the room, or are some pieces clearly redundant?
- Are displays of decorative objects threatening to take over every available surface?

This type of assessment should help you to identify where the problems lie. If it takes only a few minutes to put things straight, you don't really have a problem at all. A little untidiness is part and parcel of everyday life and, if we didn't feel free to make a mess from time to time, our homes would not be very comfortable places to be. If, however, you need to put considerably more effort into tidying up – and it's a daily battle – and if you are still not satisfied with the result after you have finished, it's time for a rethink.

Living areas are by their nature shared spaces. In family homes, everyone in the household is likely to be using the space on more or less a daily basis, perhaps in very different ways. It may well be that one person is making more of a mess (or less of an effort to tidy up) than others. If that is the case, you need to open the lines of communication, agree some house rules and make sure everyone abides by them.

OPPOSITE: The sideboard virtually disappeared from contemporary homes, as formal dining waned in popularity. Reinvented as a sleek, horizontal cabinet, it is finding new applications in multipurpose areas.

MULTIPURPOSE AREAS

The more activities a living area has to accommodate, the more critical the spatial planning becomes. The first step is to decide whether any of the present functions the area serves could be shifted elsewhere to relieve some of the pressure on space. Decanting a whole category of possessions – books, for example – can make a vast difference to the overall atmosphere and mood. Breathing space is more conducive to promoting a feeling of relaxation than pieces of expensive furniture or the latest electronic gadget. The living area should first and foremost be a place where whatever is on view is what you truly like and appreciate.

Where you have different activities to reconcile within the same living area you need to take a look at the basic layout to see whether there are any natural points of transition that could be exploited to separate one function from another. Leisure pursuits, such as watching television, listening to music and chatting to friends, can usefully be grouped in a single location. Those that require a greater degree of concentration, such as work or study, need to be segregated in some way. If your living area is also where you eat – and perhaps even where you cook – careful planning is required to prevent a descent into chaos.

Look at the way the room is shaped. If it falls into two distinct sections – for example, if it is L-shaped or if there is an archway or opening connecting two distinct halves – you have a ready means of signalling the change between one type of activity and another. Alcoves are useful places for private zones for study. If, on the other hand, there is no such in-built distinction, you will have to mark the shift yourself using furniture layout and possibly partitions and dividers.

Half-height or half-width spatial dividers are a good way of suggesting discrete areas of activity without blocking light and views. An island unit, breakfast bar or counter can form the outer 'wall' that defines a kitchen area within a multipurpose space. Similarly, a judiciously placed storage unit can provide enough enclosure to screen a study area from the more communal parts of a living room. Sometimes, furniture placement is all it takes. If you eat in the living

room, positioning a sofa so that its back is towards the dining area can make explicit the difference between the two activities; rugs can also be useful as a means of anchoring a seating arrangement and visually identifying the non-working part of the room.

There are various ways you can build in flexibility if you are very short of space:

• If the living area is the only place you can put up overnight guests, consider buying a sofa bed. Invest in the best you can afford; cheaper versions don't function well in either mode. Alternatively, folding mattresses such as futons or covered blocks of foam can serve as additional seating during the day and a spare bed at night.

• Stools double up as occasional tables or extra seats, and can be stacked out of the way when not required.

• Build in additional storage space in the form of a window seat. The space beneath can provide a useful cache for extra bedding, toys and games, or your DVD or video library.

• If you need to use the living area for eating, but floor area is limited, consider installing a built-in table that can be folded back against the wall when not in use.

• Similarly, if you need to use the living area for concentrated work, think about incorporating a pull-out desk or work station within an alcove that can be screened from view at other times.

• A trunk or blanket box can double up as storage and a low table.

STORAGE STRATEGIES

Living areas often become repositories for books, magazines, CDs, and DVDs, and, in the family home, toys and games. A neat array of shelving housing a library is far from intrusive and will not impinge in any sense on a mood of relaxation. But when storage starts to dominate – and it is in the nature of any collection, whether it is of books or CDs, to expand – the 'living' side of things can rapidly be swamped. Many of the possessions that find their home in a living area do not offer the same degree of visual pleasure as books. Built-in or concealed storage is often a good idea for CDs, DVDs and the like – items you prefer to keep in proximity to media equipment such as televisions or music systems, but which otherwise contribute little aesthetically.

As with most areas in the home, the general aim should be to keep the floor in the living area as clear as possible, which means focusing on working walls of storage. The smaller the space at your disposal, the more discreet and invisible the storage should be. Because most living areas already contain a number of large pieces of furniture, such as sofas and armchairs, unfitted storage solutions – chests, armoires, freestanding cabinets and similar pieces – tend to eat up available floor space unnecessarily. It is far better to devote one wall to organization, where it will read as a single entity, than to have a number of incidental pieces of storage furniture dotted about the place, hampering traffic routes and limiting your options for room arrangement.

An excessive reliance on containers can also compromise the look of a living area, unless, of course, the containers are shelved or used as a means of organizing the contents of a cupboard. If you stack logs neatly to one side of the hearth, you don't need a separate log basket. If you find yourself relying on a number of different baskets or boxes as a handy means of clearing magazines and papers from view, it may discourage you from tackling the back issues on a regular basis.

Shelving

The mainstay of living room storage, shelving options include open shelves fixed to the wall, freestanding storage units, or shelving within concealed cupboards. Shelving is a supremely practical solution for storing and organizing many different types of

ABOVE: The television dominates most living areas these days and contributes very little aesthetically, particularly when switched off. Flat-screen TVs that can be mounted on the wall are less intrusive, particularly when concealed behind sliding panels. Here panels also conceal shelving for tapes and CDs, while drawers set into the base plinth provide additional storage.

RIGHT: This living area and workspace remains airy and uncluttered despite the vast amount of books on display.

appearance and atmosphere of an area devoted principally to relaxation. Many contemporary designers have turned their attention to shelving; such freestanding systems can provide an attractive solution in the right setting. Alternatively, consider having shelves built-in. Shelving alcoves on each side of the chimney breast makes good use of what might otherwise be redundant space, but can be a rather hackneyed approach. Shelving an entire wall, perhaps continuing shelves up and around doorways or other openings, is a more robust and architectural solution. Bear in mind that the stronger and more graphic the framework, the greater the sense of visual cohesion.

Tips for putting up shelves:

• Types of wood suitable for shelving include softwood, thick plywood, MDF (medium density fibreboard) and blockboard. Chipboard is too flimsy to take heavy loads.

• Books can weigh up to 18kg (40lb) for each 300mm (12in) of shelving. Old vinyl records weigh about 20kg (44lb) per 300mm (12in) of shelving.

• The span between shelf supports should be no greater than 700mm (28in) if you are shelving books or similar heavy items.

• Fitted shelving must be securely anchored to the wall, using rawl plugs and countersunk screws.

• Pay attention to finish and detail. You can paint wooden shelves to match the walls. A baffle or edge strip can be applied to the shelf fronts to increase rigidity and give a more substantial appearance.

• Calculate how much shelving you require by measuring the dimensions of your possessions, then adding in a generous margin for future acquisitions.

• Keep heavier items lower down, and store things that you use most frequently between waist height and eye level.

possession normally kept in living areas, from books, magazines and photograph albums to CDs and videos. Open shelves also provide a convenient place to display decorative pieces or to prop pictures and framed photographs.

In living areas, shelving must either blend discreetly with the fabric of the room or be attractive enough in its own right to bear the scrutiny. While many of us at some time in our lives have resorted to the old standby of scaffolding planks resting on bricks, rough-and-ready systems that might be perfectly adequate for organizing a workshop rarely contribute much to the overall

ABOVE: Low-level display shelving built into the fabric of this living room features sturdy wooden uprights and thick shelves, which have been painted white to blend in with the walls behind.

OPPOSITE: This robust grid of storage cubicles reads as if it were part of the architectural framework of the room and provides a good way of subdividing categories of books and magazines.

BOOKS

Books do furnish a room, as the saying goes, and the room they most often furnish today is the living room. In large Victorian country houses, the library was often used as an informal family sitting room and the association has lingered on in contemporary homes. If you do decide to keep books in a living area, whether through preference or simply because there is nowhere else to keep them, it is best to approach the matter in a wholehearted fashion. If you don't need to keep books there, instead of putting up a few stray shelves that can take only a fraction of your collection, devote available storage space to housing something else – CDs perhaps – which is more conveniently kept close at hand.

Of all possessions, I find it particularly difficult to discard books; I buy them frequently, am often given them and I write them, too, so I have accumulated a substantial collection over the years. Books not only provide valuable sources of inspiration, reference and information, but they also enshrine memories and remind one in a tangible form of the pleasure once gained from reading them.

Nevertheless, in many households, books present a real organizational problem, creeping into every room, from the cloakroom to the bedroom, overflowing from shelves and piling up on the table in the hall and on kitchen counters. In amongst the cherished volumes that you won't want to part with are bound to be copies that merit disposal, whether these are reference books that are out of date or paperbacks that you will never re-read.

Strategies for sorting:

• Discard books that you have no intention of reading again. Some people are inveterate re-readers; others would rather spend the time reading something new. Decide which type of person you are; if you are a bit of both, separate out the all-time favourites from the rest. Paperbacks that were impulse buys or a means of whiling away the hours of a long-distance flight, or those that were passed on to you by other people and haven't found their way back again, are ripe for disposal.

• Get rid of books that are obviously out of date. Many travellers, armchair and otherwise, accumulate guide books by the dozen. New editions of well-known guides come out every year, so discard the ones that are past their sell-by date. Some reference books

ABOVE: Freestanding metal shelving acts as a spatial divider. Such systems are available from commercial suppliers.

LEFT: In rooms with high ceilings there is the opportunity to extend shelving above doors, taking advantage of wall space that would otherwise go to waste.

also fall into this category, including antiquated sets of dictionaries or encyclopedias, and old atlases that might have been passed on to you by your parents.

• Dispose of duplicate books. Hang on to the best edition and discard the other(s).

• Hardbacks can be painful to dispose of because they are so expensive. However, a hardback novel that you do not intend to re-read is just as surplus to requirements as the paperback edition of the same book you were too impatient to wait for.

• Pass on books you have grown out of. Cherished editions of children's books can be handed down to your children and when they, in turn, have grown out of them, disposed of or kept in deep storage for the next generation.

• Let go of books that relate to specific achievements but which you no longer read or refer to. These may be work-related or may date from even further back, to your schooldays, for example, or your degree course.

• Discard cookbooks to which you have never referred. If you have cooked only a couple of recipes from a book, photocopy those pages and free up your shelf space.

• And, of course, get rid of books you have never read. Keeping a copy of *Remembrance of Things Past* on the shelf for ten years is not suddenly going to turn you into a fan of Proust. If you think you should read a book, but never get around to picking it up, it serves as a source of guilt. The same applies to books relating to hobbies or activities that you have never pursued in the way you anticipated.

There are many worthy homes for books that you no longer need or want, starting with family and friends – many people, in fact, operate a sort of personal circulating library, swapping new books and recommendations on a regular basis – hence the famous 'word of mouth' effect. Charity shops are another outlet, as are schools, libraries and hospitals who all welcome donations. Books that are in good condition, collections of classics, or vintage books may be worth money, and you can always consult a dealer or specialist to determine their value.

What remains of your library after you have disposed of any unwanted books should be sorted through, first according to type – fiction, non-fiction, reference – then according to size. In most homes, it makes sense to split books up to a certain extent, according to category, keeping cookbooks in or near the kitchen, reference books relating to your work in or near your study or home office, and children's books in children's rooms or playrooms. Nevertheless, the greater proportion of your book collection should be kept in one designated location as far as possible, which is usually the living room.

Strategies for storing:

• Within each principal category, group books of a similar format. If you have a large collection, further subdivision into authors or topics might be necessary. Work out a system that feels natural to you and that will make retrieval easy. In my office in the country, I use thin plywood subdivisions between different categories of books so I can easily find what I want.

• Very large books are best stored flat. Most people have limited numbers of these and it makes better use of space.

• As with any other item you are storing, keep the heaviest books on the lower shelves.

• The depth of shelves should be sufficient to support books fully. You can pull narrower books slightly forward so that all spines are aligned at the front of the shelves.

• Space the shelves so there is a gap of about 25mm (1¼in) between the top of the tallest book and the shelf above.

• Protect valuable books by storing them in closed cupboards to prevent bindings from fading in strong sunlight.

TOP: Floor-to-ceiling sliding doors with translucent panels screen recessed shelving that accommodates a television, children's board games and a CD and video collection.

ABOVE: Built-in storage should always be planned and designed according to the basic architectural character and proportions of the space. Here the low horizontal shelving that extends around the perimeter of the room complements the linear modern windows.

ABOVE: An interesting variation on alcove shelving, these floor-to-ceiling L-shaped bookcases wrap around the corners of the room, making good use of available space. A library ladder provides access to the upper shelves.

HOME ENTERTAINMENT

Back in the dim and distant days before radio, the most common item found in the average parlour or sitting room, aside from chairs and sofas, was the piano. Home entertainment has grown progressively more passive with each successive leap of technology – the present generation is more likely to press buttons or set their iPods to 'shuffle' than tinkle the ivories. Listening to music, however, remains an important means of relaxation for many people, and so does watching television.

Nowadays these activities are not exclusively pursued in living areas. Getting to grips with storage issues relating to home entertainment can take you out of the living room and into many different areas of the home, from kitchens to bedrooms, particularly if you have teenage children.

The speed of technological change has caused inevitable storage problems when it comes to home entertainment. For decades, recorded music meant vinyl. Since computerization, however, innovations have come in quick succession. Who remembers eight-track cassettes these days? Or cine film? As manufacturers phase out previous formats, we are forced to follow suit or miss out on the chance to view or hear new releases. Anyone who has visited a video rental store recently will have noticed the telltale signs that video is on the wane. Future forecasters predict that DVDs might not be far behind once the digital revolution matures into its next manifestation and all media goes 'virtual'.

The difficulty created by such rapid change is what to do with previous collections. IPods and other MP3 players now mean that it is possible to store your entire music collection in a box the size of a cigarette packet and take it with you wherever you go. Only a very few, however, have taken the opportunity this presents to get rid of all of their CDs. The tangible nature of 'things' inspires trust, which is perhaps why we are reluctant to take that final leap. And, of course, electronic equipment does go wrong – and get stolen. To suffer the theft of your iPod is one thing. To lose your entire music collection at the same time would be much more heart-wrenching and expensive to replace.

Nevertheless, keeping on top of home entertainment means facing the fact that technologies change, and by and large we have no option but to change with them. If you own the same album on vinyl, cassette and CD, you are giving the same thing houseroom three times over, as well as giving valuable space to three different types of equipment that essentially perform the same function.

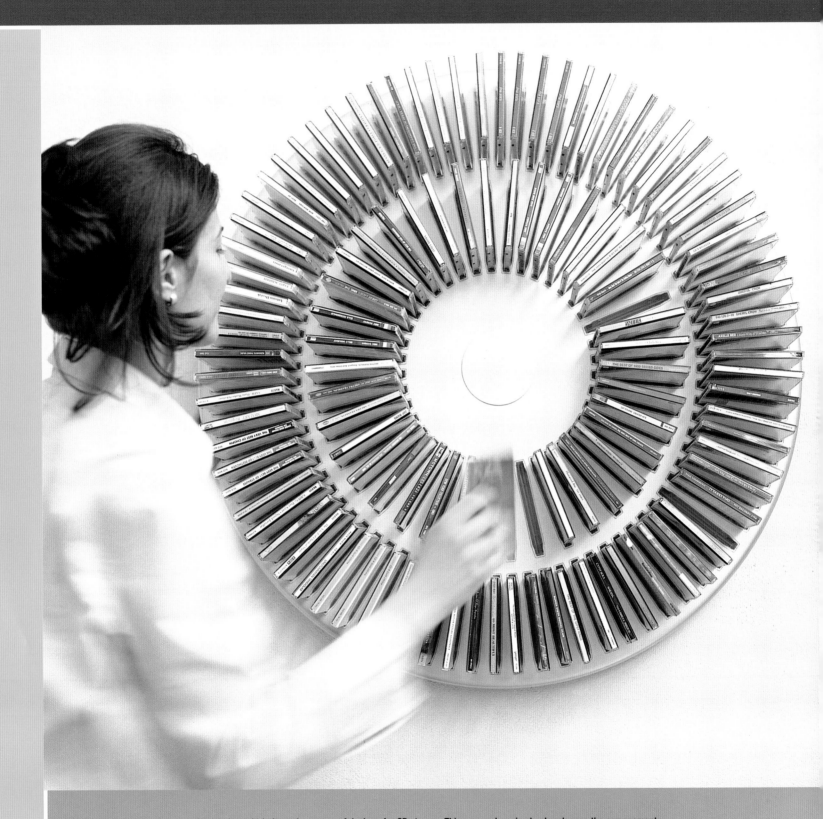

ABOVE: The arrival of the compact disc has brought in its wake scores of designs for CD storage. This carousel or pinwheel rack uses the arrangement of the CDs themselves to create a graphic effect.

Set aside some time to gather different categories of media together in one place. Videos and DVDs tend to pile up beside televisions, and if you own more than one TV you can expects piles in different locations. The same is true of CDs, which may be even more farflung – in the car, in your son's school backpack or by the CD player in the kitchen, for example. Once you have collected them together (and put them back into their cases or boxes), have a long, hard think about which you want to keep and which you are prepared to part with. If you like only one track on a CD, record it and get rid of the album.

Strategies for sorting:

• Dispose of videos and CDs that you never watch, play or even remember owning, as well as those that are broken or scratched. Many rental outlets now offer cash for 'pre-owned' videos and CDs in good condition.

• Discard duplicates, including duplicates in different formats. Choose the newest format and get rid of the other version.

• If you want to hang on to your old vinyl for nostalgia's sake, but don't play it very often, remove the collection from your living room. Vinyl is heavy and bulky. Better still, investigate how much money you might make by selling it on eBay or to a second-hand record shop – you may find the answer persuades you to get it out of the house altogether.

• Many people tape television programmes to watch at a more convenient time – and then don't. Unless you are very orderly and make a careful note about what you have taped, you will waste precious time winding and rewinding to find the programme, only to discover it has been taped over. Don't buy new blank tapes as a matter of course. Reuse old ones until the quality has begun to deteriorate, then get rid of them.

• Pass on children's films, videos and computer games once your children have grown out of *Bambi*.

• Put videos and CDs back into their boxes once you have played them to keep them in good condition.

• Rather than automatically buying a new release, think about renting it first. Buy a personal copy only if you are desperate to see the movie again, and it has shot into your Top Ten.

Strategies for storing:

• Both videos and CDs can be kept either on shelves (open or concealed behind cupboards) or in containers of some sort. CDs don't look too bad out on view, but videos leave a little to be desired.

• Store or shelve your favourite CDs, DVDs and videos near media equipment, where it is visible and to hand. The rest of the media library can go into labelled containers. This makes retrieval easier.

• Many trolleys or stands that have been designed for TVs, video recorders and CD players incorporate racking where you can keep your favourite tapes and discs.

• Set up a dedicated media zone so that you can control cabling. Don't live in a dish of spaghetti carbonara.

ABOVE: Brightly coloured CD boxes mounted on a wall, with sliding panels that conceal CDs from view. **OPPOSITE:** It is a good idea to store CDs near media equipment where they will be used. You do not need special racks or towers: drawers, shelves, boxes and other types of containers can all serve as CD storage, provided that whatever arrangement you adopt makes it easy to locate what you want.

MEMORABILIA

Mementoes of family history, pictorial or otherwise, give our homes meaning and a sense of personality. In many households, however, these sentimental items accumulate at a greater rate than our capacity to organize them, review them and gain any pleasure from them. And because of the emotions attached to these items, a certain ruthlessness is required to restore order.

Endless rolls of photographic film snapped while on holiday that have never even made it to the developers, home videos of birthdays and other celebrations, unsorted snapshots dating back so far you that are not sure of the date – all comprise another category of possession that can spiral out of control, compromising the space at your disposal. When this threatens to happen, the emotion attached to such belongings is not a pleasant sense of nostalgia but a persistent and nagging guilt.

In theory, there is no particular reason why photograph albums and home videos need to be stored in the living area. In practice, however, this is where many people do choose to keep them, simply because looking through a photo album or watching a home movie is more enjoyable when the experience is shared with other people. In addition, if you store such items out of the way and out of sight, you are unlikely to revisit your memories very often.

Getting to grips with memorabilia is a rainy day activity that can be made less daunting if you enlist support and help from other family members. Dig out all of your old photographs or video tapes and clear space on a table where you can get down to some serious sorting.

Strategies for sorting photographs:

• Equip yourself with enough albums to take about a quarter to a third of your collection. This will give you an incentive to edit your photographs down to a more manageable number. Matching albums always look better on display than a collection of different sizes, types and colours.

• Sort photographs into years, then into events or categories. Spread all the photographs of your holiday, for example, out in front of you and keep only the ones that are sharp, interesting or tell the story. If you tend to holiday in the same place every year, you will find the same scenes cropping up.

• Once you have decided which pictures are worth putting in the album, get rid of the others and the negatives.

• Use the process of sorting to learn ways to improve your photography. Some people take too many pictures; others take pictures too quickly.

• Think about displaying the best images in enlarged form.

• Be just as ruthless when it comes to digital photographs and digital videos. Images take up a vast amount of memory on your computer. Choose the best pictures and burn them onto CDs to free up your desktop.

Care and maintenance

Once you have set up proper storage systems in the living area it should be easy to maintain good order and to keep it clean. Living areas rarely need the type of intensive daily cleaning that kitchens and bathrooms, for example, require. Weekly vacuuming and dusting can be supplemented by more intensive cleaning from time to time.

• Clean wooden furniture with beeswax once or twice a year. Avoid using spray polishes, especially on old furniture, as it can create sticky residues and destroy precious patina. Beeswax is also good for removing white rings caused by setting down wet glasses.
• Dust books and ornaments regularly. In Georgian times, the tip of a goosewing was used to dust books. You can use a feather duster, or the soft brush attachment for cleaning upholstery that comes with your vacuum cleaner. Always dust from top to bottom, and shake out dusters outdoors once the dust has built up.
• When vacuuming, don't forget the areas under furniture or around skirting boards (baseboards) where dust tends to accumulate. Vacuum carpets and rugs at least once a week.
• Pay attention to handles, light switches and door frames, which tend to get grubby with fingermarks.
• Clean windows can make a huge difference to the way a room feels and to the quality of natural light. Find a reliable window cleaner if you don't want to tackle the job yourself.
• Every few months dismantle and clean light fittings. If fittings can't be removed, clean them carefully in situ.
• Clean loose covers and curtains periodically, either in the washing machine if they are washable, or have them dry-cleaned.

How to tackle spills on carpets and rugs:
• Mop up excess liquid immediately using an absorbent cloth or paper towel. Don't rub or you will force the stain further into the pile.
• Don't add additional liquid or you will spread the stain.
• Once you have blotted the area, wash gently moving from the outer edge of the stain towards the centre, but avoid overwetting.
• For oil-based stains use solvent or dry-cleaning fluid.

• For water-based stains, use a gentle solution of water and mild detergent (such as detergent for hand-washing wool or silk), or use a carpet shampoo.
• For spills that contain both water and oil (such as tea or coffee with milk or cream) wash with detergent first. When the area has dried, use dry-cleaning fluid.
• Never apply salt to wine stains.

OPPOSITE: Don't allow piles of photographs to build up. Once you have had your pictures developed, put them straight into an album.

BELOW: Unobtrusive media storage allows living areas to remain places of relaxation. If your TV is concealed when not in use, you will watch less.

STORAGE SOLUTIONS
FOR LIVING ROOMS

ABOVE: Sturdy, inexpensive and portable, log baskets can be used for many purposes other than storing logs – to hold magazines and papers, for example, or as a toy box. **BELOW LEFT:** Glossy coloured metal cabinets come in various shapes and sizes, and bring a sleek contemporary style to living-room storage. **BELOW RIGHT:** A simple and understated magazine rack consists of a springy curve of bent cherry wood.

ABOVE: Storage containers come in a range of colours and materials. ABOVE RIGHT: The Isokon Penguin Donkey, designed in the 1930s by Jack Pritchard and Egon Riss, is so-called because it has four legs and two panniers. It is made out of bent plywood. BELOW LEFT: A perfectly poised long, low storage unit-cum-coffee table in sleek polished metal. BELOW RIGHT: This mobile unit in MDF could be used either for storage or display, or as a room divider.

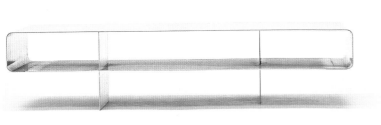

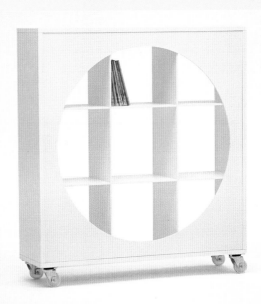

CASE STUDY: ONE-SPACE LIVING

Multifunctional or one-space living demands careful planning, not only to make the most of the available area, but also to allow each distinct activity to be performed efficiently and practically. Where separate functions overlap or encroach upon each other, there is the risk of confusion and muddle. If they are kept too distinct, however, as in conventional room-by-room layouts, much valuable space can be sacrificed. At the same time, storage needs to be properly considered, with the relevant equipment and possessions kept readily to hand.

This multipurpose area occupies the attic of a former coach house in Utrecht. The principal intention behind the conversion was to retain as much of the original character of the building as possible, while accommodating a range of diverse activities – sleeping, washing and working – within the same circumscribed space. The solution adopted here was to enclose not only storage areas, but also different activities themselves within box-like enclosures. The function of the space as a whole changes depending on whether the boxes are opened or closed.

This solution was partially influenced by the fact that the sleeping area is for guests only and is therefore not in constant use. While a separate guest room would have eaten into the available floor area, the guest 'box' is a snug compartment that fits neatly into the overall

layout. One entire wall of the box lifts up to fold flush against the sloping ceiling, using a rope and pulley. Other enclosures house clothes storage and a washing area. These, too, are similarly discreet.

Open storage space is devoted to an extensive library, arranged on built-in shelving to either side of a large window in the end wall. The shelves are extended right into the eaves to take advantage of every last bit of space. To one side of this library-cum-home office is a sitting area, well lit by a large window set into the plane of the roof.

Decorative choices underscore the precision and clarity of the spatial planning. The main beams and roof structure are left exposed to provide a strong sense of the original architectural character. Dark stained floorboards throughout help the space read as a whole. The storage enclosures themselves are made of solid pine, painted white on the outside and varnished on the inside.

ABOVE, LEFT TO RIGHT: When required, the entire front of the guest 'box' is lifted up using a rope and pulley. A sitting area is tucked into one corner of the library. The storage and functional enclosures are made from solid pine painted white. One enclosure houses a washing area. **RIGHT:** An extensive library occupies the end wall of the attic.

CASE STUDY: LIVING ROOM

ABOVE AND RIGHT: In my own living room, shelves cantilevered from the walls and painted white so they are less obtrusive hold a collection of disparate objects that I have collected over the years. When you are arranging a display area, spend some time playing about with different groupings to achieve some sort of visual balance.

My own house in the country bears evidence of two conflicting sides to my nature. On the one hand, I am passionate about clear, uncluttered space and prefer to live in surroundings that are as light and airy as possible. On the other, I do like beautiful things. By beautiful things, I do not mean objects that are necessarily of great monetary value or that have so-called investment potential, I mean things that have character and charm, that have some innate natural appeal or that speak to me in some way.

In my living room, I have attempted to reconcile these two preferences – for uncluttered space and for the sheer aesthetic pleasure that beautiful objects can bring into one's life – by making the walls a display area for some of my favourite things. I am fortunate to have a big enough house so that my books can be housed elsewhere, which leaves the living room free to serve solely as a place for relaxing. The neat array of objects lined up on their white shelves reinforces this peaceful, contemplative mood. Were the same things to be scattered around the room on tabletops and mantelpieces, the effect would be much more cluttered, perhaps even claustrophobic. Instead, pushed to the background, the collection reads to some extent as if it were part of the structure of the room.

When you are setting aside an area for display, the way in which you decide to display the objects in question is just as important as which objects you choose to put on view. I like the hands-free quality of these shelves, with concealed fixings that give the impression that the shelves are floating in space. I also like their robustness. If you are displaying objects of any weight, shelving needs to be sturdy enough to bear the load. But thin shelving, in any case, can look rather edgy, as if it might topple down any minute, whether or not there is any risk of such a thing happening. Chunky shelves have a more pleasing presence and substantiality. Although these shelves are thick, they are painted white so that they blend in with the walls.

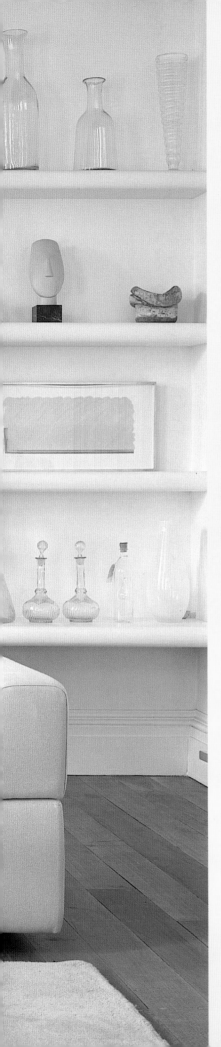

LEFT: In order for a display area to read as a coherent entity there should be some basic affinity between the objects or pictures on display. While what is on view in my living room shows quite a degree of variety, there are also similarities – a relatively restrained palette of colours, natural materials and a certain quirky irregularity that betrays objects made by hand. I am not an inveterate collector – I tend to acquire or get given things individually – but I do have a passion for glass.

4. Kitchens and Eating Areas

The kitchen plays a multitude of roles. As the place where food is prepared and cooked on a daily or thrice-daily basis, it is the hardest-working area in the home. As the informal centre of family life, it is also a social hub and may well be where you eat most, if not all, of your meals. In addition, kitchens serve as store rooms for a wide variety of disparate items, from pots and pans to spices and frozen food. Good storage systems are not only essential when it comes to the efficiency with which you perform daily routines, but are also an important means of maintaining your health and preventing sickness. If your kitchen knives are rattling around loose in a drawer with other utensils, they will quickly become blunt. If fresh food is improperly stored, however, you run the serious risk of food poisoning.

OPPOSITE: Whichever approach to storage that you choose will determine the appearance of your kitchen to a large extent, as well as affecting how easy, or otherwise, it is to perform basic everyday tasks.

ASSESSING YOUR NEEDS

The organization of your kitchen should reflect the way you live. Consider how well your kitchen is supporting your daily routines in order to identify areas where change is overdue. Tastes alter and you might find yourself gravitating to a new type of cooking that demands different equipment and ingredients. Or you may be cooking less often. Either way, it is a good time for review.

• How long does it take you to find things? Do you have to hunt for the whisk or the can opener every time you want to use it? Do you know without opening cupboards where you keep the cereal, spare light bulbs or garbage sacks?

• Have a look at the worksurface. Is it clear or cluttered up with gadgets, provisions and extraneous items? How much of what you keep out on the counter is actually waiting to be put away somewhere else or hardly ever used?

• Are there any provisions or utensils out on view that you do not use every day?

• Do you keep equipment and provisions near where they are regularly used?

• How much fresh food do you throw away every week? Are there items in your refrigerator, freezer or store cupboards that are long past their use-by date? Do you often buy duplicate food items when you go to the supermarket?

• When you come back from shopping, do all your food purchases fit in cupboards, or are you forced to leave items out on view until they are used up?

• Are there any gadgets in your kitchen that you never use or use only once a year or so? Likewise, are there dishes, glasses or pieces of kitchen equipment that are used very infrequently?

• Is it easy for you to access the interiors of all of the cupboards and drawers? Do cupboard doors cause an obstruction when they are open?

• What additional roles must your kitchen serve? Eating area, laundry room, administrative hub, playroom?

• Do items accumulate in the kitchen that have nothing to do with the activities that take place there?

• Is the kitchen the first port of call for family members when they return home?

Once you have made a thorough review of your space, set aside some time to sort through all the different categories of kitchen possessions and foodstuffs, discarding whatever is surplus to your requirements. By doing this, you may well find that you regain a significant proportion of available storage space and free up most of the worksurface.

Many people imagine that they need a bigger kitchen when what they really need is simply to make better use of the one that they already have. New kitchens are expensive and disruptive to install. If yours is not functioning as efficiently as it should, a few hours of concentrated reorganization and improved shopping habits might make all the difference.

ABOVE: A sleek contemporary kitchen with discreet built-in storage opens out on one side to connect to an outdoor eating area.

ABOVE RIGHT: A larder cupboard has sliding doors made of translucent glass so the contents are visible, but slightly obscured. A wall-mounted rack houses magazines.

RIGHT: The entire wall behind the sink and preparation area slides back to reveal shelving for kitchen appliances and other essentials.

ABOVE: The first stage in kitchen planning is to come up with a workable layout that suits the space at your disposal. An arrangement such as this double island layout needs plenty of floor area.

KITCHEN LAYOUTS

Whether your kitchen is mainly built-in or contains unfitted elements, there will inevitably be fixed points in the layout corresponding to servicing arrangements – electrical supply, gas supply (if any), fresh water and drainage. Kitchen planning entails coming up with a layout that incorporates these fixed points in an efficient and workable manner.

The notion of the 'working triangle' informs kitchen planning. This concept specifies that the kitchen should be laid out with reference to three essential points: the refrigerator (or cold area), the hob (cooktop) and oven (or hot area) and the sink (or wet area). Cooking and preparing food is a sequence of related activities. If the three points of the working triangle are spaced too far apart, you will waste time and energy producing even the simplest meal. If they are too close, your working conditions will be cramped and awkward, and might even be dangerous. Ergonomic studies recommend that the total distance travelled between the three critical points should be no greater than 6m (20ft).

The working triangle can be applied to several different types of layout. These include the single-line layout, where the three points are arranged along the length of a wall; the L-shaped layout; the U-shaped layout; the galley kitchen; and the island kitchen. Island kitchens require the most floor space, while single-line and galley kitchens are more efficient if you do not have much room to play with.

Storage should be considered in the context of the working triangle. Begin planning the organization of your supplies and equipment by concentrating on the critical area between the sink and the stove. Anything you keep within arm's reach of this hard-working area should relate directly to preparing and cooking the kind of food that you eat on a regular basis. Here is the place to store the pots and pans you use almost every day, frequently used utensils, basic provisions and condiments, as well as cleaning products such as washing-up liquid and dishwasher powder. Be guided by your own tastes and cooking preferences. If you hardly ever bake, you don't need to keep flour in this part of the kitchen; if you don't use the food processor very often, don't keep it on the kitchen counter.

The remainder of your provisions and equipment can be stored away from the main preparation area, organized according to type. Keep all tinned, preserved and dry goods in a larder cupboard. Store cutlery (flatware) and crockery close to the kitchen table to make setting it easier, but not too distant from the sink or dishwasher. Specific items of equipment or small appliances that you use from time to time, such as blenders and food processors, need their own dedicated storage area.

Organizing a kitchen on the basis of accessibility is no more than common sense, yet all too often people make things harder for themselves than they really need to be.

ABOVE: Curtains and blinds make a cheap, simple and impromptu means of screening storage areas.

LEFT: Cupboards need customization to some degree; these box shelves are just the right size for storing sauces and condiments.

FAR LEFT: The framework of these built-in cupboards is strongly expressed, giving a robust sense of architectural character to the kitchen.

CUPBOARD SPACE

Cupboards and drawers are basic kitchen containers for a wide range of provisions, equipment and utensils, as well as cutlery (flatware), crockery and glassware. It does not really matter whether the storage space is built-in or freestanding – the basic principles of maximizing the use of the available space are more or less the same.

Most of these principles involve customizing the interiors of cupboards and drawers, so that what you keep inside them fits better and is easier to retrieve. Many kitchen manufacturers produce a number of accessories and fittings so that you can tailor storage space to your needs and requirements. Others have ingenious ways of wringing the maximum space out of built-in units – the revolving corner cabinet is an obvious example, while shallow drawers slotted into kickplates or plinths are a relatively new trend.

How much you squirrel away into cupboards and drawers depends to some extent on your tastes and preferences. Those who find it more calming to work in an uncluttered environment tend to keep all but the most basic kitchen items and provisions concealed from view; others find open shelving more inspirational and welcoming. Bear in mind, however, that most types of non-perishable food will last longer if they are not exposed to direct light and the heat of the kitchen, while dishes and glasses can get dusty and greasy if they are not behind closed doors. Glass-fronted units can give you the best of both worlds in the latter case (Perspex, or Plexiglas, is too static for kitchen use).

• Subdivide drawers to organize cutlery (flatware), utensils and basic supplies such as garbage sacks, light bulbs and spare fuses.

• Vary shelf height and depth so that you can group similar packages or items in the same location – cereal packets on one shelf, for example; canned goods on another.

• Make use of the backs of cupboard doors to store items that might otherwise be overlooked – such as pan lids, or a collection of herbs and spices.

• Think about how cupboard doors open. 'Easy-on' hinges that allow doors to open so they are plumb with the frame are neater than conventional types. If space is very tight, consider changing hinged doors to those that slide or lift up and over, or to tambour doors that roll up like a shutter.

• Investigate the variety of interior fittings on the market. These include wire or basket trays for keeping root vegetables aerated, trays that keep bread moist, and separate bins for deep drawers that enable you to store bottles upright.

• Within a run of storage units, it is best to include a block of drawers, rather than having a drawer at the top of each unit. The uppermost drawer can be used to keep utensils and other items on daily call.

ABOVE: This ingenious fitted kitchen storage includes a deep drawer at the base for storing dishes and plates, with another cupboard above the built-in oven accessed via a door that pulls up and over.

DISHES, GLASSES AND CUTLERY

If your kitchen serves as an eating area, provide storage for everyday dishes, glasses and cutlery (flatware) near the table so that it is easy to lay. You may also wish to keep table napkins, tablecloths and place mats in the same location.

Storing crockery and glassware on shallow shelves allows you to find what you need easily, minimizing breakages and chipping.

• Discard any plate, dish or glass that is cracked or chipped. Chipped dishes are not only unsightly, but are also unhygienic, as chips and cracks can harbour bacteria.
• Stack plates and bowls in short piles of six to eight, according to size and pattern. Alternatively, keep your plates in a rack, either positioned directly over a draining board or within a cupboard. Racking plates prevents them from scraping against each other.
• Glasses should not be stored upside down on their rims. Group them by size and type.
• Many people like to hang cups and mugs from hooks. Bear in mind, however, that this is not a good idea for delicate china. The handle is a cup's weakest point.
• Drawer dividers are essential for organizing cutlery (flatware). Keep silver flatware separately from stainless-steel cutlery, preferably in felt-lined canteens. Silver tarnishes when exposed to light and humidity. If you do not use silver regularly, keep it in felt bags.
• In many homes, the dishwasher is effectively where crockery and cutlery is stored. Get into the habit of emptying the dishwasher after the cycle is over. Bear in mind that delicate or hand-painted china may not be dishwasher-proof. The same is true of knives or cutlery with bone or wooden handles.

OPPOSITE: A country-style built-in cupboard features drawers below shelving for cutlery and crockery.

TOP: Plate racks are a good idea for dishes in everyday use. Position them so that plates drain onto a draining board or into the sink.

ABOVE: This cupboard provides storage for the sink as well as the dishes. Doors fold back to either side and slot neatly away.

RIGHT: Dishes can also be stored in the drawers of units. Sort crockery into like with like and keep piles no greater than six to eight items.

LEFT: A bright yellow circular shallow wall cupboard makes a graphic feature of kitchen storage and a striking contrast to the professional-style fittings and fixtures.

BELOW LEFT: A hanging rail positioned above that country kitchen stalwart, the Aga, keeps everyday utensils within easy reach.

OPPOSITE, LEFT AND RIGHT: An ingenious space-saving idea for small kitchens: these gas hobs (cooktops) hinge back and are hooked in place so that they can be suspended flat against the wall when not in use, freeing up additional counter space.

COOKWARE, UTENSILS AND SMALL APPLIANCES

Part of the pleasure of cooking is having the right tools for the job. Serious cooks gain serious

pleasure from whisks, measuring spoons, knives, peelers, spatulas, ladles, sieves and colanders,

and the rest of the batterie de cuisine. Utensils and other cooking equipment can proliferate,

however, until their usefulness is compromised by the amount of storage space they devour,

no less than the time you may have to spend locating them in a drawer or cupboard.

• Get rid of any gadget, utensil or small appliance that you no longer use. We all succumb to such impulse buys from time to time, beguiled by the promise of labour-saving or flushed with enthusiasm for making pasta, bread or ice cream. Ask yourself when you last used the fish kettle, and if you can't remember, free up the space in your cupboards for cookware you do use.

• Stack pans inside each other and store the lids separately, perhaps in a rack on the back of a cupboard door.

• Suspend any utensils that are in daily use from a hanging rail or a wall-mounted rack, or keep them in a subdivided top drawer near the hob (cooktop) or sink.

• Store kitchen knives in knife blocks, which have separate slots for each knife, on a magnetic strip or in a shallow drawer by themselves. Always wash kitchen knives by hand.

• Keep small appliances that you do not use every day off the counter, either in cupboards or in an appliance garage. If you make fresh juice every morning for breakfast, the juicer can stay on the worktop, but there is probably no need to keep the mixer there.

FOOD

Different types of foodstuff require different keeping conditions to maintain flavour and prevent spoiling. Furthermore, keeping conditions change once the state of food is altered – when cans are opened, or when food is cooked or defrosted, for example.

The contemporary convenience lifestyle has left many people ignorant of the basic rules of food hygiene. A single bacterium can multiply a million times within seven hours and cause a serious stomach upset, or worse. At the same time, if you are constantly finding food in the refrigerator that is past its use-by date, you will be losing money on a weekly basis. To prevent waste, review your shopping habits.

Take the time to go through all the areas – refrigerator, store cupboard, larder or pantry – where you are storing food, and discard any that is out of date. All foods have a life span, including preserved and canned foods. You should also throw away any food that has been hanging around for a while simply because no one likes it. Adjust your shopping list accordingly so that you buy only what you eat and eat what you buy. Leftovers are rarely revisited.

In this context, it is also important to review your approach to those items that you buy in bulk. Bulk buying that has been inspired by discounted price or special offers – the 'buy one, get one free' strategy adopted by many supermarkets – makes sense only if you actually consume that particular type of food on a weekly or daily basis. Otherwise, you will just end up creating a storage blockage that you don't need.

A well-stocked kitchen is a welcoming, hospitable place. It enables you to rustle up something different for supper when everyone's getting a little tired of your favourite dishes, and it also allows you to produce a meal when the unexpected happens and family or friends drop by unannounced. As someone who spent the greater part of his childhood in the austere war and ration years, I like the sense of plenty that well-stocked kitchens provide. However, when 'plenty' shades into excess and packets start falling off the larder shelf, it is time for a review.

Fresh food

The home for most types of fresh food is the refrigerator. Perishable food keeps for longer in cool conditions, which means that you will have less wastage between shopping expeditions. Stuffing the contents of your shopping bag into the fridge, however, is not enough to maintain food in proper condition. There are a number of basic rules to follow.

• Do not overstock your refrigerator. This can cause the temperature to drop, which means items will not remain fresh for as long as they are supposed to. The temperature inside the refrigerator should be no warmer than 5°C (41°F). You can check the temperature with a fridge thermometer.
• Don't position the refrigerator near heat sources, such as ovens and hobs (cooktops). This can compromise operating efficiency.

ABOVE: Many people store all their fresh food in the refrigerator. While certain types of fresh food, such as meat and dairy products, do need to be kept cool or they will perish rapidly, fruit and vegetables can lose their flavour and texture. If you are going to be eating vegetables, particularly root vegetables, within a day or two, you can keep them out of the fridge in a cool, dark location.

• Defrost the refrigerator at regular intervals, according to the manufacturer's instructions.

• The warmest zones in the refrigerator are the crisper tray and the door. The crisper tray provides ideal keeping conditions for salad ingredients and vegetables, while the door generally includes racking for storing eggs and less perishable condiments.

• Take food out of plastic packaging and plastic bags, otherwise condensation will build up and promote decay.

• Raw food should be kept separately from cooked food to prevent cross-contamination. Cover or wrap raw meat, fish and poultry, and keep it on the lower shelves away from cooked leftovers.

• Cooked leftovers should also be kept in sealed containers. Cooked food should never be put directly into the refrigerator when it is hot; allow it to cool for a maximum of one hour.

• Food that has a pungent flavour, such as cheese, should be kept in a separate box or lidded compartment to prevent the flavours from transferring to other food.

• Mop up any spills in the refrigerator as soon as they occur, and clean it out properly at least once a week.

• Refrigeration affects the taste and texture of some fresh ingredients. If you intend to use vegetables within a day or two, keep them out in the open to maintain their flavour. Root vegetables, such as onions and potatoes, can be kept in wicker drawers out of direct light.

• Bread can be stored for short periods in earthenware crocks or special bread drawers.

Stock provisions

This broad category of foodstuffs ranges from store cupboard essentials, such as floor and cooking oils, to canned food and preserves, herbs and spices. Unopened packages, cans and jars will keep for a considerable period of time without deterioration; once the contents are exposed to air, however, they will need to be either decanted into sealed containers or stored in the fridge.

• Check the date stamps. Even canned food has a life span. Discard whatever is well and truly past its use-by date.

• Don't keep more than a month's worth of basic non-perishable provisions on hand.

• Arrange your larder cupboard(s) so that the provisions that are consumed or used most frequently are the most accessible. Don't bury things away in the cupboard. Arrange cans and jars so that you use the oldest first.

• Keep a few provisions that you use every day on an open shelf or on the countertop. You can keep these in storage containers if you don't want the packaging on view. Use up what is in the container before replenishing the supply.

• Decant the unused portion of an opened can into a separate container, store it in the refrigerator and consume it within two days. Never store food in opened cans.

• Dried herbs and spices that are kept for too long lose their flavour and bite. Those you do not use very often should be kept out of direct light in a cool, dark cupboard. Racks fitted to the back of cupboard doors can be a good way of organizing herbs and spices, as small bottles and containers can get pushed to the back of shelves and forgotten.

• Always keep shelves clean and dry. Spilled food, especially cereals, will attract mice and other pests.

Frozen food

In theory, frozen food can be kept almost indefinitely. In practice, three months is the maximum keeping time if the food in question is still going to taste of anything. Food that is frozen for too long often shows what is known as 'freezer burn'. These white patches indicate a deterioration of texture and flavour.

Much will depend on the type of freezer that you have. Freezer compartments in refrigerators are given star ratings that indicate how cold they are and hence how long frozen food can be safely stored in them. Some freezer compartments can be used only for storing food that is already frozen; others can be used for freezing fresh or cooked food.

To earn its keep, a freezer should be used chiefly as a way of keeping food for slightly longer than would otherwise be possible if it were kept in a refrigerator. They are also particularly helpful if you live in a remote area and are not able to shop for supplies very frequently, or for freezing garden produce.

• Unlike refrigerators, freezers work best if they are well stocked. However, they should be defrosted periodically – always follow the manufacturer's recommendations.

• Don't use the freezer as a dumping ground for leftovers that you are unlikely to use up, but haven't the heart to throw out. That is just a way of postponing the decision.

• Ice-cube trays can be a good way of freezing home-made stock or special sauces and curry pastes.

• Never refreeze defrosted fresh food without cooking it first. Defrost all frozen food in the refrigerator, allowing one to two days, depending on the weight and type of food or product.

• Label and date home-frozen food clearly. Food should be frozen in rigid, sealed containers or in freezer bags from which as much air as possible has been excluded.

• Think about siting your freezer elsewhere in the home to free up kitchen space. Separate chest or upright freezers can be positioned in basements, utility rooms or garages with no great compromise to basic working efficiency.

The larder

With the arrival of the refrigerator, the dedicated larder or pantry all but disappeared from the average home. If you have an appropriate area that could serve as a larder, however, it is well worth investigating this storage option.

The larder or pantry is a room or cupboard that is well ventilated and slightly chilled by natural refrigeration. Traditionally, in houses in the northern hemisphere the larder is sited on the north-facing side of the house and has at least one external wall (in the southern hemisphere, the south-facing side of the house is coolest). A stone floor and slate or marble shelving helps to keep the temperature sufficiently cool to store a wide range of foodstuffs, including vegetables, fruit, preserves, game, ham, sausages and salamis. With the entire space lined with shelves, it is easy to assess your food supplies at a glance; larders also provide space for keeping wine and bulk stores.

An alternative to the separate larder or pantry is the pantry cupboard. Those available from kitchen manufacturers often have double doors that open to reveal an interior subdivided by shelves, racks, bins and baskets.

Traditionally, the larder was also accompanied by the scullery, a separate room apart from the kitchen where dishes were washed and stored. If you have a similar adjoining area, this can be a good place for the dishwasher.

LEFT: Even a small cupboard or closet can be fitted out as a larder. Here provisions are neatly arranged on shelving, while deep drawers provide space to store canned goods. A larder is also a good place to keep bulky appliances that you do not use every day.

OPPOSITE: Natural refrigeration can be aided by positioning the larder on the north-facing side of the house. Ideally, at least one wall should be external and the space should be well ventilated. Stone, slate and marble used on floors or shelves also help to maintain cool conditions.

ABOVE: A serious wine collection requires proper storage. This spiralling cellar simplifies retrieval. There are a number of companies that produce ready-made cellars that can be slotted into a basement void.

The wine cellar

If you keep only a few bottles on hand for immediate drinking, you don't need specialized wine storage. Simply rack the bottles in an accessible location well away from heat sources such as ovens and hobs (cooktops). In my apartment at Shad Thames, I have wine racks in the toilet upstairs. The room is dark most of the time – it has no window – and it is close to the kitchen area for easy retrieval. It also makes the toilet more interesting to use.

If you are a wine buff or collect wine for investment purposes, you need a proper cellar in a cool, dark location. Years ago, an acquaintance of mine was given a pipe of port for his twenty-first birthday. Twenty-one years later, when he decided the moment had come to sample the vintage, he discovered the bottles had all turned to vinegar. He had been keeping them in the attic.

Wine that is laid down for a number of months or years needs to be kept at a temperature of 11°–14°C (52°–57°F). It should be laid on its side so that the wine keeps in contact with the cork and the sediment settles. Some companies produce proprietary wine cellars that fit in basement voids; these often take the form of spirals that are accessed from hatches in the floor. You can also buy special wine storage units that fit under the worktop like a fridge; these, however, will take only a limited collection. Whatever method you choose, ensure that you keep records of what is stored where so that you do not need to disturb bottles unnecessarily.

ABOVE RIGHT: For the wine buff more interested in the enjoyment of wine than in its investment potential, racking bottles in an accessible location is a good solution.

RIGHT: Older properties may have useful basement areas that can be given over to wine storage. Basements tend to be naturally cool, providing ideal keeping conditions.

faced with a heap of dirty dishes, it can be very demoralizing. Leave chores such as oven-cleaning for too long and you will be faced with an uphill struggle. Learn to clean up as you go along to reduce the amount of effort you have to put in.

• Don't use scouring pads or abrasive cleansers on glass or stainless steel. Wipe over frequently with a damp cloth and a little washing-up liquid, and dry with a paper towel. Dulled stainless-steel surfaces can be revived with the application of a little baby oil or WD40.

• Bicarbonate of soda and vinegar are two store cupboard basics that can be used to tackle stubborn residues. Vinegar mixed with a little water will lift burnt deposits from saucepans and casseroles. To remove baked deposits from the oven, dust the surface with bicarbonate of soda, sprinkle with a little water, and leave overnight.

• Store bleach and chemical cleaners well away from food cupboards. If you have young children and keep such products in a base unit, invest in a childproof lock.

Waste disposal

Kitchens generate a good deal of waste – everything from potato peelings to plastic packaging. To keep pests away, it is a good idea to remove organic and food waste every day. Massive kitchen trash cans may seem more convenient than smaller bins which cannot hold so much, but you will inevitably empty them less frequently. A small bin will not only force you into a better disposal routine, but can also fit inside a base unit, keeping the floor area clear. There are also bins that can be attached to the rear of cupboard doors.

In many areas of the world, it is mandatory to recycle and sort household waste. Even if you do not live in such an area, it makes sense to get into the recycling habit. Separate your rubbish into colour-coded containers: one for glass bottles and jars, one for metal cans, one for paper and one for organic waste. Organic waste can go onto the compost heap, or you can dispose of it with a waste-disposal unit fitted to your sink. If doorstop recycling collection is not available where you live, you can take the containers into which you sorted the waste directly to recycling banks.

Care and maintenance

Kitchens require a great deal more care and upkeep than other rooms in the home. Thorough cleaning of key areas on a daily basis is necessary. While the floor may need a wash only once a week, it should be swept daily. Hobs (cooktop) and worktops need to be wiped down as soon as they are used to prevent a build-up of grime. There is no law that says you shouldn't leave dirty pans to soak overnight, but if every time you come into the kitchen you are

OPPOSITE: White has long been a popular choice for kitchens because spills show up readily, prompting more regular cleaning. As this example shows, all-white does not necessarily result in a clinical look.
RIGHT: A self-effacing kitchen contained within warm wooden cabinets. The stovetop and sink are covered with a lid when not in use.

Dealing with pests

Common pests that are attracted to the kitchen include flies, ants, mice and rats. Any such problem tends to indicate that your food storage is substandard or that you are not disposing of kitchen waste properly or fast enough. Nevertheless, pests do get in from time to time, particularly during the warmer months when doors and windows are left open.

Flies can be deterred by keeping food properly covered and stored at all times and bins or trash cans emptied regularly. Rather than use a fly spray (which includes toxic chemicals) you can obtain environmentally friendly alternatives that make use of the type of pungent natural odours such as lavender that flies find repellent. In the case of ants, you will need to track down the nest and get rid of the problem at source.

Where mice are concerned, prevention is often easier than cure. Once mice are in residence, they can spread to other areas in the home, and they do breed and proliferate at an incredible rate, spreading diseases through their droppings and urine. Remember that a crumb is a meal for a mouse. Spillages in cupboards, on shelves and around bins, if not tackled immediately, can result in unwelcome house guests. The first sign of mice are droppings (small, black and about ½cm/¼in long) in cupboards and other recesses. Other signs include a musty smell, squeaking and scratching. Once you have a direct sighting, you know the problem is well and truly out of hand.

• Keep everything in the kitchen spotlessly clean and empty dustbins and trash cans regularly.
• Block up any gaps or holes where mice or rats could get in.
• As long as you don't have pets or small children, put down poison in special trays.
• Other types of trap include the standard sprung mousetrap or glue traps. Bait traps not with cheese, but with strong-smelling food such as tuna or peanut butter.
• Get yourself a good mouser. Cats can clear up a mouse problem in no time at all. Once there is a cat living in your home, the mice won't come back again.
• Alternatively, call in pest control.

STORAGE SOLUTIONS FOR KITCHENS

ABOVE: Cupboards in the base of a curved counter provide a convenient storage space for crockery. **BELOW LEFT:** Many kitchen suppliers produce special fittings and accessories for customizing unit interiors, such as this deep drawer for wine storage. **BELOW CENTRE:** A freestanding metal unit designed for racking bottles. **BELOW RIGHT:** Unfitted kitchen furniture includes pieces such as this wooden trolley on castors. As well as storage, it provides an additional worksurface.

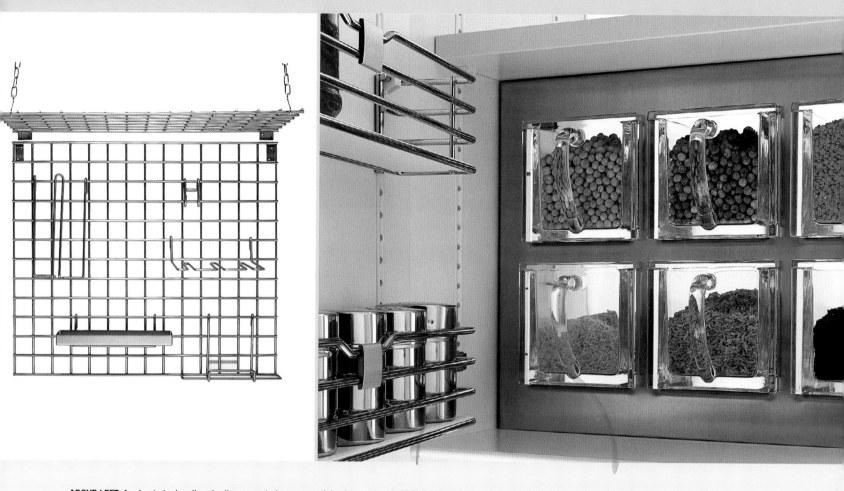

ABOVE LEFT: A robust steel wall rack allows you to keep essentials close at hand. **ABOVE RIGHT:** See-through glass containers mean that contents can be read at a glance. **BELOW LEFT:** Heavy-duty steel trays make retrieving crockery much easier. **BELOW CENTRE:** Separate colour-coded bins facilitate the recycling of household waste. **BELOW RIGHT:** Kitchen displays – fruit and vegetables in basic bowls and baskets – contribute a sense of warmth and hospitality.

LEFT: While the outer wall of the kitchen island is uninterrupted, the inner face is fitted with a row of cupboards and appliances.

CASE STUDY: KITCHEN

Kitchens are the hardest-working areas of the home and demand several different levels of storage. Items that are used frequently need to be close at hand, preferably within easy reach of the main preparation areas. Equipment and utensils on less frequent call, along with those that do not provide much in the way of visual interest, should be organized into closed cupboards reasonably near to where they will be used. Where the kitchen also doubles up as an eating area, there will also be the need to store crockery, glassware and cutlery (flatware), preferably within easy access of both the table and the kitchen area itself.

In this kitchen, with its fine architectural detailing, appearance matters as much as practicality. The sleek contemporary lacquer and stainless-steel island and base units have a chic understated elegance that makes a subtle contrast to the room's existing period mouldings, cornicing and architraves. A steel rail provides a hanging display of batterie de cuisine. The island separates the preparation area from the table in front of the window. Plantation-style adjustable shutters diffuse natural light. This juxtaposition of old with new is far more effective than attempting to replicate the original period style in the design of kitchen cabinetry.

ABOVE: The 'outer' face of the island screens kitchen activity and built-in appliances. An undermounted sink and flush hob (cooktop) leave the surface of the island unit uninterrupted. A hanging rail directly above the worksurface means that essential everyday equipment is right where it is needed.

LEFT: Panelled doors conceal shelves and drawers for storing crockery, cutlery and serving dishes. The scale of the cupboards, as well as their architectural detailing, makes them read as part of the structure of the room. The cupboard doors are the same size as the door into the kitchen.

5. Bathrooms

In recent years, bathrooms have emerged as an area of the home where people are prepared to spend considerable sums of money. That is not surprising. The more hectic and stressful our daily lives are, the more important the bathroom becomes as a personal refuge and centre of relaxation. However, while people are increasingly devoting greater space to bathrooms and wet rooms, such areas still largely remain among the smaller spaces in the home. Storage must be carefully planned, both to make the most of available space and to preserve a peaceful restorative atmosphere.

Like the kitchen, bathroom layout is determined by fixed points of servicing. Because there tends to be slightly less floor area, built-in storage is often a good solution, an approach that also allows you to integrate the sink, toilet, bathtub and shower in a neat and considered way in order to make the best use of any given space.

OPPOSITE LEFT: A backlit glass cabinet for storing towels is a feature in its own right. **OPPOSITE RIGHT:** A wall-hung vanity cabinet with a sink mounted on top maximizes the sense of space. Such pieces give bathrooms a more furnished and less clinical look.

ASSESSING YOUR NEEDS

Storage is well down on the list of the functions a bathroom must serve, but it is nevertheless important to consider storage requirements early on if you are planning to put in new fixtures. At the same time, thinking about what you keep in the bathroom can help you to discard the redundant items and make a better use of existing space. This is particularly the case when it comes to shared or family bathrooms.

• When was the last time you sorted through your bathroom cabinets? If the answer is more than a few months, you may be hanging on to cosmetics, medicines and other products that are past their use-by date. Old medicines and remedies may be harmful. Most cosmetics have a shelf life of about six months or so. Past this time, some will dry out and deteriorate; others, particularly creams applied with the fingers, may become unhygienic.

• Are shelves and ledges around the bathtub crammed with shampoos, conditioners and bottles of bath oil? If every member in the household has their own preference when it comes to basic grooming products, your bathroom will begin to resemble a pharmacy. You may have tried a product, then decided you didn't like it. Discard anything that is half-used and likely to remain that way.

• Are cleaning products out on view? It is a good idea to keep basic cleaning products at hand in the bathroom, but a bottle of bleach is not a very attractive prospect when you are lying in the tub.

• Is the bathroom a dumping ground for towels in varying states of dampness or cleanliness?

• Do you have to clear the tub of plastic ducks and boats before you can have a bath?

• Does your bathroom serve as a utility area as well? Do you need to keep the washing machine there, or could it be sited elsewhere?

• If you are sharing the bathroom with the rest of the family, how easy is it for everyone to identify their own towels, toothbrushes, flannels (washcloths) and so on?

• If your teenage daughter monopolizes the bathroom for protracted grooming sessions, it may be worth providing her with a make-up area in her bedroom where she can preen to her heart's content.

• If you are considering installing a wet room, have you thought about where you are going to keep the articles that you would otherwise store in a bathroom? Unless your wet room is very large – and most are not – everything from toilet paper to towels is going to get damp.

Everything you keep in the bathroom should be either directly related to the activities that take place there or in more or less daily use. Bulk supplies of toilet paper and other products should be kept out of the bathroom altogether. What you do keep in the bathroom should fall into one of two categories: the things you don't mind having on view and those that are better concealed.

ABOVE: Beautifully detailed bathroom storage provides open shelves for towels and is neatly integrated with the long, trough-like sink.

ABOVE RIGHT: A freestanding divider separating bedroom from bathroom provides wall space for storage cabinets on the bathroom side. The light and airy quality of the room is preserved because the divider does not extend right up to the ceiling.

RIGHT: A sink is sited in a recess within a seamless storage wall.

STORAGE APPROACHES

Built-in storage represents the most popular option for bathrooms. For good reason: fitted storage gives the bathroom a unified architectural look, it conceals pipe runs and the underside of sinks, and at the same time it provides useful space for stowing away a wide variety of miscellaneous bathroom essentials that are best kept hidden from view.

Vanity units may be wall-hung or raised on legs to keep the floor area clear and enhance the sense of space. Tall, shallow wall cupboards make the most of narrow recesses and alcoves. Another alternative is to opt for wall-hung toilet pans and sinks, hiding the cistern, soil pipe and plumbing runs behind a dummy wall that also incorporates storage space. Similarly, enclosing a bathtub in a panelled framework creates a look of solidity and provides additional shelving space at the head and foot, as well as cupboards hidden behind the panels.

As with any fixed layout, you will probably require expert help to come up with the optimum arrangement of space and make sure everything fits and functions as it should. If you have a generous amount of space to play with, you might consider moving the tub into the centre of the room, for example, or siting it at right angles to the wall, to create a more dynamic arrangement than the typical perimeter-hugging layout generates.

Freestanding or unfitted pieces of storage furniture generally take up too much room to find a ready home in the average bathroom. If you have a very large bathroom, however, armoires, chests and other such pieces will go a long way to providing a more furnished look, which can help bathroom fixtures and fittings from appearing as if they were stranded in space. Such pieces can house the bulk of your bathroom possessions, from towels to spare toilet paper and cleaning products. Be careful, however, not to store cosmetics, bath products and bathroom cleaning agents directly on wooden shelves where drips and splashes might cause stains. Group them in an intermediate container first.

Open shelving is a good idea for products and accessories that can bear the scrutiny, as well as those items you need to keep within arm's reach. Glass shelving is less intrusive in a relatively small area and can be wiped over very easily if spills or splashes occur. Otherwise, you can make use of vanity tops or ledges surrounding built-in features to collect together a (limited) group of containers or products. Many bath and beauty products come

OPPOSITE: The bathroom shown in these pictures is a little larger than average, which makes a combination of storage approaches possible. While the open shelves for stacks of spare towels under the bowl-shaped sink are built-in, the armoire against the opposite wall is freestanding and provides capacious storage for a range of bathroom accessories and products that are better kept behind the scenes.

ABOVE LEFT: Many of the products, lotions and potions that are used in the bathroom can be kept on shallow shelves. These glass shelves, neatly integrated into a narrow built-in cupboard, are easy to keep clean and do not discolour or stain in the same way as shelves made of wood.

ABOVE RIGHT: An antique towel horse is an elegant detail in a period-style bathroom.

LEFT: A long, low vanity unit mounted on a wall provides generous storage space. The overall sense of space is enhanced because the unit does not extend right down to the floor.

OPPOSITE LEFT: Tongue-and-groove panelled cupboards painted white have a charming simplicity, in keeping with the country setting.

OPPOSITE CENTRE: An old table with barleytwist legs has been adapted to make a double vanity unit with bowl sinks sunk in the top.

OPPOSITE RIGHT: An alcove in the corner of a wet room houses a washing machine and clothes dryer stacked on top of each other. The alcove is screened from view by a simple curtain.

in beautiful packaging and require no concealment at all. Those that do not can be decanted very simply into glass jars and lidded containers. As with kitchen displays, try to stick to the same basic type of container. If your bathroom is on the small side, avoid baskets and raffia containers that may deteriorate in hot and steamy conditions. They can look a bit tacky, too.

Many bathroom storage accessories reflect a certain coyness about bodily functions. I can well remember the custom of concealing toilet rolls in baskets; scarcely better than stowing them away under the frilly skirts of a doll dressed up as a flamenco dancer. Toilet-roll holders come in a range of materials; chrome, ceramic and brushed-steel versions impart a sense of quality lacking in their plastic counterparts.

Storage specifics:

• Bathrooms are not necessarily the best place to keep all your bath towels and linen, as conditions may be damp and steamy. If the bathroom is small, you are unlikely to have sufficient room in any case. Try to keep the bulk of your towels elsewhere, in an airing or warm linen cupboard; alternatively, store them away from wet areas within the bathroom itself.

• Wall cabinets that combine storage space with a mirrored surface and integral lighting make a good use of available space.

• Keep toothbrushes by the sink, suspended in a wall-mounted toothbrush holder or similar, so that they can drain after use. Standing toothbrushes upright in containers, such as mugs or glasses, is unhygienic and will result in a foul sludge collecting at the bottom. Colour-code the toothbrushes in a shared bathroom to make sure everyone knows which one is which. Electric toothbrush heads come with removable coloured plastic rings to ensure easy identification.

• Shaker-style pegboards mounted on the wall or the back of the bathroom door can be used to hang up dressing gowns or bathrobes, or to suspend individual spongebags or cosmetic bags.

• Keep soap on a wire rack or in a perforated or ridged dish so that it doesn't sit in a sticky puddle between use.

• Bathroom trolleys make an attractive means of storing spare towels and bath products. They can be pulled near the tub when required and pushed back out of the way again afterwards.

• Always keep medicines and toxic cleaners under lock and key if you have young children. Some medicines need to be kept in cool conditions, which means out of the bathroom altogether.

• Plastic mesh bags make good containers for bath toys; otherwise you can buy caddies that slip over the side of the bathtub.

• Heated rails organize towels, as well as giving off a considerable degree of background heat. One recent variation on this theme consists of a box with an open front that you mount on the wall. The box is heated, which keeps towels warm and dry.

• If your bathroom doubles up as a laundry room, provide a place to keep soap powders and fabric conditioners hidden from view, as well as a laundry basket.

• Bath racks, in chrome-plated metal or wood, which bridge the sides of the tub, allow you to keep essentials within reach. They are also handy places to prop a book.

• Bear in mind that good ventilation is essential in a bathroom.

LEFT: A rough-and-ready concrete bench with shelves below has an elemental simplicity. Such fixtures can be cast in situ by a specialist subcontractor.

BELOW LEFT: Shallow plastic pull-out trays provide a good means of organizing a variety of bathroom accessories. In family bathrooms, or where the bathroom is shared, it is often best to allocate separate storage for each bathroom-user.

OPPOSITE: These galvanized aluminium boxes provide a way of storing bathroom products and accessories that is well in keeping with the rustic aesthetic.

Care and maintenance

Any shortfall in basic cleanliness is immediately apparent in the bathroom. Together with the kitchen, it should be the most regularly and intensively cleaned area in the home. Frequent cleaning not only keeps the room pleasant to use on a daily basis for everyone in the family, but also ensures that you do not have to put so much effort into cleaning, as grime does not get a chance to build up. The less you put on display in the bathroom or leave out on view, the easier cleaning becomes.

• Clean hair out of sink, bathtub and shower drains and plugholes. Failure to do so can cause a blockage – or worse, an overflow that does real damage. Pouring boiling water down the drains from time to time can help prevent blockages from building up due to soap scum – and save you a fortune in plumber's bills.
• Choose the appropriate cleanser for the task to be done, and

for the material of which the fitting is made. Abrasive, scouring cleansers should not be used on acrylic bathtubs or on glass or stainless-steel sinks. Clean stainless-steel sinks with a proprietary product designed for that purpose or use mild detergent and dry with a paper towel. To restore shine, rub with baby oil. Some glass sinks have a coating that makes them resistant to spotting, but they do demand extra maintenance to remain looking good.
• Don't leave wet shower curtains bunched up or they will become mouldy – leave them pulled closed until they are dry.
• Clean tiles regularly to keep grouting looking fresh.
• A solution of vinegar and water is a good way of removing limescale from shower doors and tiled surfaces.
• Use special toilet cleaners or thick bleach to clean the toilet, and brush it thoroughly to prevent the build-up of limescale.
• Natural scents from essential oils are far more refreshing and welcoming in the bathroom than the synthetic odours of commercial air fresheners; they are also better for you and the environment.

STORAGE SOLUTIONS FOR BATHROOMS

ABOVE: Lavatory humour – an improvised toilet-roll holder complete with cork stop. **BELOW LEFT:** There is a wide range of bathroom cabinets on the market, from simple mirrored units to more expensive designs incorporating lighting, shaving points and other features. This double cabinet has sliding mirrored doors.
BELOW RIGHT: A variation on the standard bathroom shelf, this design consists of a chrome rack onto which oak boxes and shelves can be slotted.

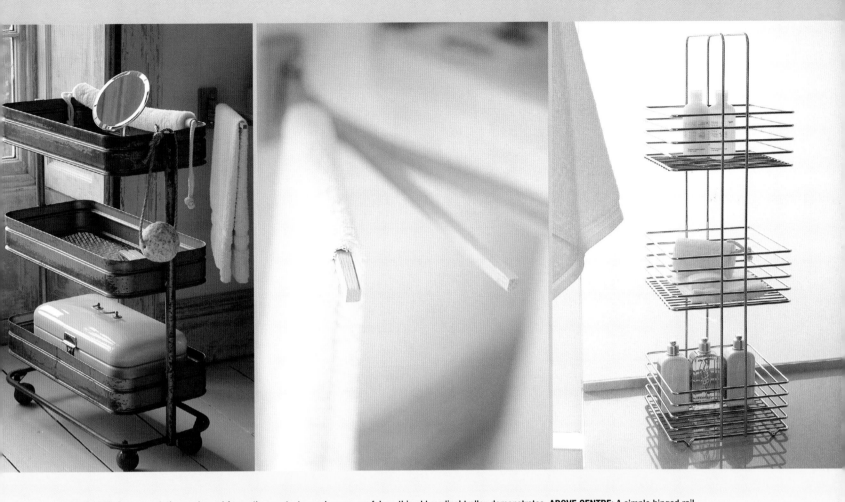

ABOVE LEFT: Storage solutions salvaged from other contexts can be very useful, as this old medical trolley demonstrates. **ABOVE CENTRE:** A simple hinged rail with three wooden arms keeps towels aired. **ABOVE RIGHT:** A portable tiered stand makes a good home for bathroom products. **BELOW LEFT:** A similar concept to underbed storage – this tub has storage space on one side in the form of open boxes and drawers. **BELOW RIGHT:** A wire shelf bridges the corner of a shower.

CASE STUDY: BATHROOM

Lofts, with their generous proportions and robust architectural character, throw up certain practical and aesthetic challenges. In the case of this bathroom, located in an old sweet (candy) factory that has been converted into apartments, the main requirement was to come up with a design that was more human in scale, without losing the expansive quality generated by the high ceiling and large windows.

The bathroom occupies part of a bedroom. To create an element of intimacy and enclosure without sacrificing the openness and fluidity of the space, the lower portion of the wall was clad in stained oak panels. The panelling not only helps to suggest a more human scale, but also provided the means to build in concealed storage. In addition to a pivoting

mirror over the double sink, there are cubbyholes and cupboards behind sliding panels where bathroom products and accessories are stored. When the panels are closed, they read as an integral part of the space.

In decorative terms, the rigorous opposition of black and white has a certain timeless quality, while the stained oak adds depth and textural character. The bathtub, raised on teak supports, and the double sink were both reclaimed from a grand hotel dating from the early twentieth century. The chrome taps (faucets), shower set and towel horse have a similar retro appeal. In keeping with the loft aesthetic, the pipework is exposed, running the length of the floor in an aged oak channel. The wooden floor is stained to match the panelling.

6. Bedrooms and Dressing Rooms

Of all the areas in the home, the bedroom is where we expect to find a little peace and quiet. We spend roughly one-third of our lives sleeping and the very least the bedroom should provide is comfortable and tranquil surroundings where we can wind down at the end of the day, as well as a pleasant environment in which to wake up refreshed the next morning. All that is really required to meet those needs is a good bed, sensitive lighting and perhaps sound insulation.

In most households, however, the bedroom is also called upon to serve as a storage area for the bulk of one's wardrobe, housing everything from shoes to jewellery, evening wear to accessories. Without careful planning, the storage function that the bedroom must often play can begin to impinge on its essential role as a personal refuge.

OPPOSITE: Halfstairs, leading up to a roof terrace, provide storage space for a wine collection and a place to display photographs when not in use. The hollow headboard is used for stowing away blankets.

ASSESSING YOUR NEEDS

If you have no option but to store clothes in your bedroom – a practice Le Corbusier famously denounced as 'unhygienic' – the greater part of the assessment process will focus on your wardrobe and how it is organized. Many diverse belongings creep into bedrooms, however, and you may be surprised what review brings to light about your preferences and habits.

• Can you close your wardrobe doors easily? Are the drawers filled to bursting and the rails packed so tightly that it is difficult to locate what you want to wear?

• Are clothes left out on a regular basis, draped over chairs?

• Is there a dedicated area for storing shoes, or are these kicked off and left where they fall, or jumbled up at the bottom of your clothes closet so that it's hard to find both halves of a pair?

• What do you keep at the bedside? If you like to read in bed, is there a place to keep books and magazines, or are they simply piling up on the floor? How many of them have you read?

• Is there a television in the bedroom? If so, are there also heaps of videos and DVDs strewn about the place?

• How clear is the floor? How easy is it to move about the bedroom? How easy is it to make the bed?

• Are there belongings in the bedroom that are waiting to be taken elsewhere? Some people open their mail in bed; others read the morning paper there. Many people enjoy breakfast in bed from time to time. Are there letters lying about which need to find their way to your desk, or old papers which should be in the recycling bin?

• Do you keep valuable items under the bed? A lot of people do and for that reason it is the first place a burglar will look.

Begin by clearing out of your bedroom any possessions that have no legitimate right to be there. Then set aside a good few hours for getting to grips with the contents of your wardrobe. If you are going to find it difficult to make decisions about what you should keep and what you should dispose of, ask an honest friend or family member to help you. They may also be pleased to give a home to some of your unwanted items.

OPPOSITE LEFT: Many people like to keep objects and pictures of personal significance on view in the bedroom, as well as in more public areas of the home. Here shelves recessed into the wall double up as a display area and a place to keep books for bedside reading.

OPPOSITE RIGHT: Clothes storage has been separated from the sleeping area, visually at least, simply by suspending tab curtains from a metal rail. The dressing area features a hanging rail and a selection of containers, rather than traditional storage furniture.

ABOVE: A combination of open and closed storage – deep drawers and hanging rails projecting out at right angles from the wall – have been installed in an alcove in a bedroom.

RIGHT: A properly organized wardrobe makes it easier to get dressed. Regular review is important to prevent closets or hanging rails becoming overcrowded with clothing that you no longer like or wear – or that no longer fits you.

CLOTHING

It has been estimated that most people wear only 20 per cent of the clothing they own. This means that, unless you have a vast dressing room or walk-in closet at your disposal, your clothes storage is likely to be more overcrowded than it needs to be, and a good proportion of that space will be wasted. Overhauling your wardrobe so that you end up only with clothes you really like and that suit and fit you, discarding the rest, is no less emotionally difficult than any other form of clutter control (and possibly more difficult, as self-image comes into it), but it is an essential first step.

Strategies for sorting:

• Get rid of anything you have not worn for a year or more. Some people hang onto clothing because they expect a trend might come back into fashion. Fashion is indeed very cyclical, and vintage has never been more popular. The older you get, however, the less likely you are to revisit your previous fashion statements.

• Throw out clothing that does not fit you. Reviewing your wardrobe is painful because the process has a tendency to throw up reminders that you promised yourself that you would lose a bit from your waistline. Discard those guilt-making items, and if you do shape-shift in the future, celebrate with a new purchase.

• Get rid of clothing that doesn't suit you. Unflattering clothing is bad for your self-esteem.

• Discard any pairs of shoes or boots that don't fit you. You may be prepared to tolerate a crippling pair of heels on occasion, but

some people have a tendency to talk themselves into buying shoes that don't fit if a pair in their size is not in stock. Get rid of the offending articles. They are bad for your feet – and your feet are not going to change size.

• Discard items you bought on impulse but didn't much like when you got them home. People are often blinded by bargains and lose all grip on their fashion sense. Just because a dress is fabulously reduced and has a famous name on the label does not mean it needs to be in your wardrobe.

• Throw out the waifs and strays: lone socks, shoes, earrings or any other article that was once part of a pair but is no longer, as well as accessories such as belts that are specific to outfits that you no longer own or wear.

• Separate any items in your wardrobe that require minimal repair from damaged clothing that would be prohibitively expensive

to restore. I am all in favour of mending whenever possible and I don't mind a little wear and tear, but some clothes can get to the point where they are beyond rescue.

• Set to one side all clothing that will not be required for the next season or two. This is obviously easier in parts of the world where the weather follows predictable yearly patterns. Even in Britain, however, where winters can be mild and summers chilly, at least some seasonal rotation of clothing is possible. Storing out-of-season clothing away from the bedroom or dressing area frees up useful space and provides better keeping conditions for your immediate wardrobe.

Strategies for storage:

• Never use wire hangers, except for shirts that you wear frequently. Use wooden hangers or padded ones for delicate items.
• Knitwear, which includes knitted dresses, sweaters and shawls, should be folded and stored flat either on shelves or in drawers.
• Store eveningwear and formal suits inside hanging cotton garment bags, and make sure they are clean before putting them away if they are not to be worn for some time.
• Hang clothes of a similar type, length or colour together. Hang skirts from tape loops or use sprung hangers that can be inserted into the waistband of the garment. Hang trousers (pants) from clip hangers, suspended from the cuff.
• Allow a depth of at least 600mm (2½in) for hanging storage. Double-hang half-length articles such as jackets, shirts and skirts to make the most of space.
• Use drawer dividers to separate small items such as knickers (panties) and socks or keep them in separate containers.
• Don't fill drawers or stack shelves above two-thirds of their depth.
• Rack shoes on rails at the bottom of your wardrobe or closet. Alternatively, store them in cubbyholes, shoe tidies, boxes, fabric bags or lidded containers under the bed.
• Use wooden shoe trees so that shoes keep their shape.
• Pad handbags with tissue so they retain their shape, and keep in them in dustcover bags.
• Narrow rails attached to the back of cupboard doors provide a good way of storing belts, ties and scarves.
• Never keep valuable jewellery in the bedroom. Keep it in a safe or at the bank. The rest of your collection that you wear on a regular basis is best stored in a box with subdivided compartments so that like can be put with like, or in a fabric roll. Fine chains, which can become knotted if left lying loose, can be stored individually in fabric envelopes or rigid boxes.

Storage approaches

Only a very small proportion of your clothing should be kept out on view. While clothes rails have been popular for some years, this type of open storage does not provide the best conditions for keeping clothes in good order. Clothes on open rails are exposed to dust and sunlight, which may cause them to fade, and are more susceptible to moth attack. The bulk of your wardrobe should be kept in chests of drawers or similar pieces of storage furniture, or in some kind of built-in storage arrangement.

Many traditional items of storage furniture are designed to house clothes. These range from freestanding wardrobes to chests of drawers, blanket boxes and trunks. The unfitted look has its modern variants, too, in the form of recycled retail or commercial lockers and display units, as well as clothes rails and basic self-assembly storage units. While there is nothing intrinsically impractical about this means of housing your wardrobe, unless you have a large bedroom, a collection of storage furniture can begin to encroach upon the available floor space. As the bedroom is necessarily dominated by a large piece of furniture already, built-in solutions can often provide a better solution and one that is far less visually intrusive.

Fitted clothes storage systems vary widely in style and quality. Mass-market versions tend to sit uneasily between the truly architectural solution and the freestanding piece. Behind the flashy fronts, detailing and structural frameworks may be flimsy and substandard. There are companies that specialize in producing more upmarket clothes storage systems, many of which can be customized to individual requirements. Interior features may include shoe bins, adjustable shelving and portable laundry hampers, as well as drawers, hanging rails and cubbyholes.

For a sleek and seamless look, it can be a good idea to have fitted clothes storage built to your own specification. As with working walls in living areas, it is best to devote an entire wall to a built-in

OPPOSITE LEFT: Reclaimed fittings and furniture from retail stores, such as this glass-fronted display cabinet, work well for clothes storage.
OPPOSITE RIGHT: Only a small proportion of your clothing should be stored on a hanging rail, where it will inevitably be exposed to sunlight and dust.

ABOVE LEFT: Plain shoeboxes are good for storing shoes – but labelling them or sticking a photo on the box will make retrieval easier.
ABOVE RIGHT: An entire wall of this bedroom/workspace has been given over to shelving for books. With the rest of the decoration pure white, the effect is far from overwhelming.

LEFT: A platform bed, custom-designed, provides ample space underneath for storage. Boxes and baskets can be used as containers for additional linen, shoes and the like.

BELOW LEFT: A classic box bed, tucked into an alcove, has built-in drawers and cupboards underneath.

BELOW CENTRE: Cupboards built up on both sides of the bed and extending across form a niche for the bed.

BELOW RIGHT: Another underbed arrangement features sleek wooden drawers which are accessed from the end of the bed.

OPPOSITE: Those who like to read in bed often find piles of books accumulating haphazardly on the floor. Shelving them underneath the bed is one alternative; the soft rug makes searching for the right book more comfortable.

wardrobe or closet, making use of any alcoves and working with the architectural framework of the room itself. Extending storage right up to the ceiling tends to look better than stopping short at some indeterminate distance up the wall.

The interior of the wardrobe can be kitted out with a mixture of hanging space, both for full-length clothing and double-hung for half-length clothing, as well as shelves, pull-out trays or drawers, and racks for shoes. Full-length mirrors can be attached to the rear of closet doors, or you can mirror the door fronts to enhance the sense of space in the bedroom. Alternatively, door fronts can be made of translucent acrylic or glass, and the panels backlit.

Where space is tight, pay particular attention to accessibility. Drawers need a clearance of at least 1m (3ft 3in) in front; average-sized hinged doors slightly more. If you don't have the available floor area, options include shelving and hanging space screened by blinds, or by sliding, bifolding or concertina doors.

Simple containers make a good way of organizing small items of clothing, particularly within drawers or arranged on shelves or in modular units. These are often most useful where they allow you to read the contents at a glance – see-through plastic or wire containers prevent you from overlooking what is inside.

The bedside table tends to be where people keep the type of items that they need within easy reach – glasses of water, books and magazines, clocks and radios. In default of such a table, most of these items end up on the floor. In a small area, however, tables at both sides of the bed may not represent the best use of space. More fitted solutions – a shallow recess built into the wall or headboard, or a ledge or shelf extending behind the bed to each side, can provide a neater look while keeping the floor clear.

Don't forget to make the most of the space under your bed. There are flat storage containers on castors specifically made for underbed storage; alternatively you can buy divans with drawers in the base that can be used to house spare bedding, sweaters and the like.

DRESSING AREAS

If you have the opportunity, there is much to be said for removing clothing from the bedroom altogether. Separate dressing areas do not have to be very large or extensive to be effective. A walk-in closet or a short passageway lined with fitted closets on both sides can house most of your clothing and free up space in the bedroom itself.

More important than size is proximity. Dressing areas should be situated close to the bedroom or to the bathroom, which is where clothes tend to be taken off. You might, for example, consider converting a small spare bedroom into a bathroom with integral clothes storage in an adjoining vestibule.

Bespoke custom-built dressing areas are the height of sophistication. You may wish to commission a one-off design from a skilled carpenter, specifying exactly which finishes and fittings you require. Another alternative is to fit out a dressing area using a closet system manufactured by one of the many storage specialists. However, dressing areas can also be equipped more simply and economically with a mixture of hanging rails, drawers and shelves. Hanging space can be screened by doors, sliding panels, glazed or acrylic panels, or even ricepaper screens.

However you fit out a dressing area, remember to make it pleasant to use. A full-length mirror is indispensable, and good lighting, both of the dressing area itself and of the contents of closets, makes retrieving what you want much more straightforward. If there is room, a couple of chairs, stools or an upholstered bench will give you somewhere to perch when you are putting on shoes.

OPPOSITE: A small area immediately adjacent to a bedroom has been fitted out as a dressing area, complete with seating. Subtle lighting above the discreet built-in closets creates a relaxing mood.

BELOW: Small rooms can be given over to clothes storage and usefully serve other functions as well – perhaps doubling up as a spare bedroom when guests come to stay.

RIGHT: Specially made wardrobes on castors provide a flexible solution to clothes storage in an open-plan loft, as well as a means of subdividing space.

BELOW RIGHT: Bespoke dressing rooms are top of many people's wish lists. When children fly the nest, you may find yourself in a position to rethink the way in which you use different areas of your home.

Care and maintenance

Once you have organized your wardrobe, the next step is to ensure clothing remains in good condition for as long as possible. If it is stored in the wrong wrong way or exposed to the wrong type of environment, fabrics and knitted materials are vulnerable to fading, discolouration, sagging and moth attack. In the right conditions, clothing can last for years.

• Use a clothes brush to remove surface dirt and hairs.
• Never leave clothes in plastic bags after dry-cleaning. Remove the garment from the packaging to let it air, and hang it on a hanger or store it flat, as appropriate.
• Spot cleaning with dry-cleaning fluid will save you money in dry-cleaner's bills.
• Delicate clothing, and clothing made of leather, satin, lace and similar materials, requires specialist cleaning. Don't entrust such items to your local dry-cleaner.

Preventing moths

Moths, or more accurately moth larvae, can decimate a wardrobe. Unfortunately, they tend to have rather good taste, preferring the finest wool and cashmere over synthetics – once you have seen how moths shun the Gap in favour of the Gucci, you will believe they can read. A serious moth attack can result in the loss of your most expensive and treasured pieces. If you see moths flying about, it is too late – it is the larvae that do the damage.

What attracts moths are the proteins in natural fibres, as well as the fat and food residues on your clothing. A single soiled sweater, or even one that has been worn only once, stored with a clean sweater, can mean that both are attacked. You can go a long way towards preventing moth damage by ensuring that you launder or dry-clean all items, particularly woollen ones, before you put them away. If you see signs of moth damage, remove all affected garments completely. Make sure you keep closets and wardrobes clean and uncluttered.

Moth repellents:

• There are a wide range of chemical-based treatments on the market, many of which have the familiar, strong camphor odour that clings to clothes and is not particularly pleasant. These proprietary products include insecticide sprays which need to be applied along skirting boards (baseboards), between the carpet and the wall, and small sachets of repellent for placing in drawers or inside the pockets of hanging clothes. Sachets need to be replaced annually.

• Cedarwood is a traditional natural moth repellent with a far preferable odour. Because cedarwood, whether solid or veneer, is oily, it should not be placed in direct contact with clothing. Blocks can be fixed to the tops of cupboards or underneath shelving.

• Other strong- but pleasant-smelling natural repellents include: nutmeg, cloves, cinnamon, thyme, rosemary and lavender. Small tied cloth bags filled with one of these herbs or spices can be tucked into drawers or pockets. Like chemical sachets, these are effective only for about a year.

Seasonal storage

Rotating clothing on a seasonal or summer/winter basis is often a good idea. Clothes that are stored for a long period of time need to be kept somewhere that is dry and well aired.

• Before you put clothes away into long-term storage, launder or dry-clean them.

• Once clean, clothes can be wrapped in acid-free tissue paper and folded into storage boxes, trunks, suitcases or acid-free storage boxes. Make sure containers are mothproof.

• Store hanging clothes in cotton garment bags. Pillow cases and small duvet covers can be also used for long-term storage. Add lavender bags or moth repellent.

• Airtight vacuum bags are a great way of storing out-of-season clothes, as well as bulky items such as duvets and eiderdowns. Air is extracted from the bag using a vacuum-cleaner hose, reducing bulk by up to 75 per cent.

STORAGE SOLUTIONS FOR BEDROOMS

ABOVE: Worn or dirty clothes are best kept in aerated containers. These lidded baskets feature cotton liners to prevent snagging. **BELOW LEFT:** Clear plastic drawer dividers allow you to organize accessories and the smaller items in your wardrobe, such as belts, scarves and socks. **BELOW RIGHT:** There are many different products on the market that address the problem of shoe storage. This simple metal rack is less fiddly to use than canvas shoe tidies.

ABOVE LEFT: Modular storage systems can be adapted to a wide variety of uses, including clothes storage. **ABOVE RIGHT:** Drawers should never be overfilled or clothing will suffer and you will forget what you own. These open-fronted drawers are ideal for storing items that need to be kept flat. **BELOW LEFT:** Subdivided wooden pull-out trays allow you to keep like with like. **BELOW RIGHT:** This platform bed incorporates an integral bedside table complete with shallow drawer.

CASE STUDY: BEDROOM

This small apartment is the home of an artist-musician, a flooring designer and their young son. One of a number of apartments in a converted factory, it demonstrates the critical importance of storage where space is very limited. In the main bedroom, a wall of built-in cupboards neatly conceals the greater proportion of the couple's personal belongings, as well as providing room for an office area.

When it comes to constructing fitted storage, working with existing detail and proportion creates an integrated, architectural effect. Here, the central section of the bedroom window served as the template for the size and proportion of each cupboard unit.

Four panels on the central cupboard disguise the larger scale of the concealed desk, stool and cubbyholes for files and stationery.

The exposed framework of the cupboards is made from sections of wooden underlay. These were stained white, which blends with the woody tones to create patches of soft colour. These shades were then exaggerated on the individual panels. Each shade was chosen to complement the one next to it, with a few darker colours introduced. The subtle tonal design shifts with the light and creates a very restful atmosphere. The soft colours are not overly dominant, but they do provide a means of remembering exactly what is where.

OPPOSITE: A central cupboard houses a compact home office, with a worksurface and cubbyholes for storing files and other supplies.
ABOVE: The panels are painted in a range of soft colours that are easy on the eye.
RIGHT: The proportion of the panels was derived from the central section of the bedroom window in order to create an integrated effect.

7. Children's Rooms

When it comes to storage, family life poses one of the greatest challenges of all. If you are a parent you will automatically take on the role of organizer-in-chief, responsible not only for your children's possessions, but also for all the administrative details – homework, sports notices, choir practice schedules – that their activities in and out of school bring in tow. Flexible systems are essential from the word go to keep incipient chaos at bay.

As your children grow, you may be able to devolve some of the responsibility for caring for their possessions onto their shoulders. It is important, however, to have reasonable expectations in that regard. You cannot demand adult standards of tidiness from toddlers and young children, whose impulses are driving them in the opposite direction. By the time your children reach school age you can begin to encourage them to look after their belongings and to adopt orderly habits that will stand them in good stead in years to come.

OPPOSITE: Children enjoy special spaces such as alcoves and window seats. This bed, with two wide storage drawers underneath it, is tucked neatly into an alcove under a sloping plane of the ceiling.

AGES AND STAGES

Anticipation is the key to keeping on top of the storage requirements posed by family life. Many people make the mistake of thinking that when children are small, they do not require much in the way of storage space. Once a few Christmases and birthdays have passed, however, it will be more than evident that this is far from the case. If you do not want to share every square inch of your home with your child's possessions, you need to think ahead. Plan wisely, and the systems you adopt in the early years may well last all through childhood and require only minimal supplementation.

Babies

The prospect of a new arrival naturally brings out the nesting instinct in most parents-to-be. Before the child has even been born, many new parents will have equipped themselves with a considerable amount of baby kit, from buggies, strollers and slings to changing mats and cots. While a certain degree of preparation is essential if you are not going to be staggering around the shops with a week-old infant, test-driving the latest baby carriages, it is equally important not to overburden yourself with items that in the light of experience you will find that you don't really need. Ask other new parents which equipment and accessories they found most useful, and resist the temptation to buy the entire contents of the babycare department. Ease the strain on your budget by accepting any hand-me-downs you are offered. If you obtain a cot or crib from a friend or family member, however, do buy a new mattress.

While a baby will have not yet accumulated a huge number of toys, equipment such as pushchairs, strollers, highchairs and baby seats can be very bulky. Plan ahead and think about where you are going to keep such items so they don't end up cluttering your living areas. The pram in the hall may not be the enemy of creativity, but it makes getting in and out of the front door a great deal more awkward.

Pre-school children

Once your child has started to walk, the fun really starts. Now is the time to childproof your home – see page 187. Much play at this stage is floor-based and will continue to be so for a good many years. At this point you may wish to think about changing the allocation of bedrooms to give your child (or children) a larger area that can double up as a playroom and bedroom, which will help to

RIGHT: A child's bed is highly personal territory. This girl's bed has been turned into something of a bower with swathes of coloured net. Underbed storage is supplemented by a small bedside chest.

BELOW: Large graphic letters add a lively touch to floor-to-ceiling cupboards in a baby's room.

ABOVE: A high-level bed provides room underneath for a desk and chair. Simple storage furniture, such as the white bookcase, is versatile enough to be used for different purposes as the child grows.

ABOVE RIGHT: This custom-built platform bed includes ample workspace. Any high-level or bunk bed must be properly designed and soundly constructed.

OPPOSITE: A working wall of storage, entirely fitted out with cupboards and drawers, means that the floor is kept clear. This is particularly useful during the early years, when children's play is largely floor-based.

relieve the pressure on living areas. Two or three is the age at which most children move from a cot or crib into a proper bed, which may well dictate alterations in room arrangement. Take the opportunity to build in as much storage capacity as you can. Underbed space is just as valuable for storing children's belongings as it is in adult bedrooms. Drawers or boxes on castors make retrieval easier.

School-age children

With the onset of school life and other activities outside the home, possessions, equipment and accessories really start to multiply. This is a good time to think about integrating storage with sleeping or working areas. There are many good modular systems on the market that combine high-level sleeping platforms with desk and storage space underneath. Don't allow children to sleep in upper bunks or on high platforms until they are at least five or six. The basic structure should be robust, properly anchored, and fitted with guardrails and a secure ladder.

As games become more complicated you will need to adopt a 'sort and store' approach to keep like with like. Modular containers are extremely useful in this respect and can be improvised from a variety of discarded containers or packaging.

Children who are sharing a room need some means of keeping their possessions separate. When each child has his or her own dedicated storage area for treasured items, it helps to reduce sibling squabbles. Separate storage areas can also serve as a means of informally dividing up the space so that both children have territory of their own. Reinforce good habits by involving your children in tidying up – if you start early enough and make it a game, you stand a better chance of gaining their cooperation at a later stage.

Teenagers

Seemingly overnight your sensible, helpful child has mutated into an alien being. Most teenagers regard the floor as prime storage space, and, failing that, the rest of the house. Belongings detach

themselves from teenagers with alarming rapidity, and many disappear for good, lost in some nether world of abandoned sports kits, lone sneakers, house keys and homework folders. This is a stage when you are just as likely to find your son's best friend's T-shirt in his room as his own. While it is counterproductive and bad for family stress levels to insist that your teenager adheres to your standards of tidiness and order, it is also essential to lay down some ground rules to prevent the entire household from getting swamped.

Make the transition to teenage life as simple as possible by undertaking a full-scale review of your child's belongings to make way for the inevitable new acquisitions as interest shifts from Lego to computer games and music magazines. You may also wish to reconsider room allocation again at this stage, so that your children can have rooms of their own. Help to keep the floor as clear as possible by incorporating plenty of shelving. Provide out-of-the-way storage space for bulky items, such as sports equipment, so that they don't litter hallways or get dumped just inside the front door.

MOVING WITH THE TIMES

In general, when furnishing children's rooms, it is best to avoid buying miniaturized storage furniture and items specifically designed for nursery use. Your child will not remain a baby for long, and such pieces will rarely earn their keep. Instead, think about flexible solutions that can be adapted to each stage of your child's development.

Flexible storage solutions

All of the various types of storage detailed below are flexible enough to be put to a number of different uses as your child grows. Children grow not only in size, but also in their ability and interests, which is why versatile storage is so important. It is economic, too.

Bookcases

A freestanding bookcase provides invaluable storage for many types of possession, from a baby's nappies (diapers) and toiletries to picture books, toys and games. A decently made, sturdy bookcase will see years of use, from babyhood through to adolescence. Wide-spaced shelves are more practical than narrow ones. Make sure that the bookcase is securely anchored to the wall – many little children use them as climbing frames and could become seriously injured if the bookcase and its contents toppled over.

Built-in shelving

A more considered solution is to line a wall with shelves, perhaps mounted on adjustable brackets. A huge proportion of what children own is shelvable, including items of clothing. Boxes and other containers used to store toys and games can also be shelved. When children are small, make sure that their favourite toys or what they use daily are kept lower down, where they can reach them easily.

Chests of drawers

Another all-purpose storage solution is the chest of drawers. A simple, well-made chest is a good early purchase. When your child is very young, you can use it as a means of storing nappies (diapers) and clothes, while the top can be a useful surface for a changing mat. Later on, a chest of drawers can house the bulk of a child's wardrobe. Until children reach school age most of their clothing will not need to be hung up.

Containers

For the first year or so, you will probably find that most of your baby's toys will fit into a single container. Choose one that is sturdy and portable, so that you can tidy up easily wherever your child is playing. Soon, however, you will reach the stage where one container is not enough. Stacking plastic boxes in bright colours, wicker or rush baskets, stout cardboard boxes and similar designs are the mainstays of children's storage. Games or toys with multiple parts can be organized into containers of different colours. Containers on castors can be wheeled under the bed. A larger lidded chest can be used to house dressing-up clothes for make-believe play.

Hanging storage

Clothes rails that are placed at a low level, Shaker-style pegs and hooks on the back of the door can be used for hanging up a variety of possessions which are in frequent use. While many items of clothing in the early years do not need to be hung up, hanging storage is a good idea for dressing gowns, aprons, washbags and outdoor gear, as well as sports equipment and games kits. When your children are sharing a room, give each one a set of pegs or a rail so that they can keep their belongings separate.

Display areas

Children are not minimalists. From a very early age, most enjoy seeing their most precious possessions out on view. A dedicated display area will provide a lasting source of visual delight. A portion of wall painted with blackboard paint may help to curb a child's desire to 'decorate' the walls with magic markers. The tops of chests of drawers and open shelves are natural display areas for models and favourite toys. Consider putting up a pinboard so you can put your child's most recent creative efforts out on view, along with photographs and other mementoes.

Teenagers enjoy plastering every available wall surface with stickers, posters, pictures and magazine clippings. By this stage, a single pinboard won't provide enough surface area. Instead, you could line an entire wall with cork – or simply accept that after the collaging stage has passed redecoration will be in order.

Administrative centre

Keep important documents relating to your children, such as birth certificates, immunization records and school reports, in an accessible file. Routine or daily administration, such as notices, schedules and school letters, should be gathered together in one place – on your desk, in the kitchen or wherever you tackle household matters. A calendar put up in a prominent position can serve as a useful reminder of key dates.

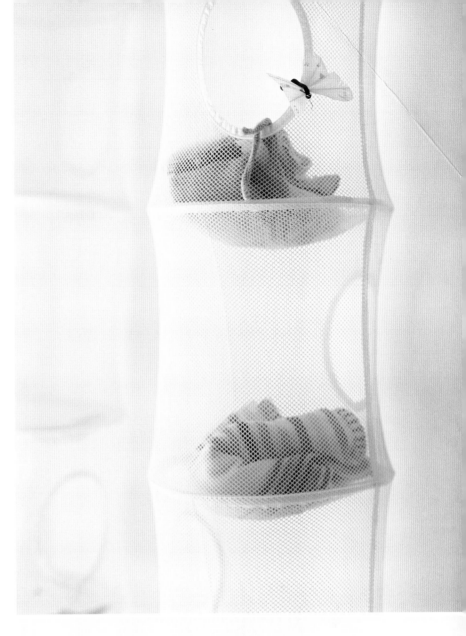

ABOVE: Hanging storage, such as this mesh tube, keeps belongings on view, but off the floor. Children enjoy being surrounded by their toys and precious possessions – in the early years out of sight generally means out of mind altogether.

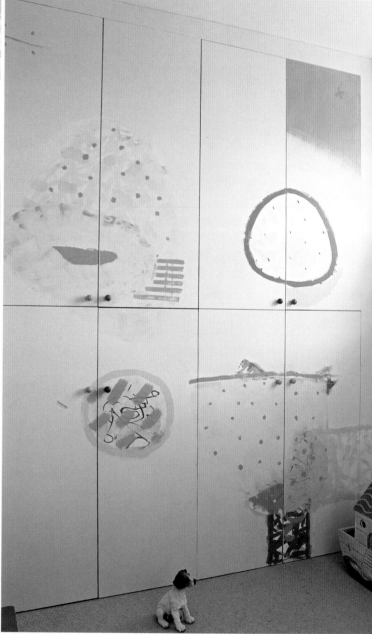

ABOVE: Making good use of what might otherwise be redundant space under the eaves, this closet has perimeter shelving for ease of access.

RIGHT: Built-in storage does not need to be bland and self-effacing. Vivid colour and cheerful decoration creates a playful effect in a child's room.

OPPOSITE: Alcove shelving extends at waist height into a worktop which is ideal for creative play.

NEW FOR OLD

The other side of the storage equation is getting rid of things. Possessions – clothing, books, toys, games, sports equipment, and so on – cycle in and out of family life at a furious pace. Children grow and develop fast, and unless you instigate regular clearout sessions you will be rapidly overwhelmed by their belongings. Frequent reviews help children to learn to let go of possessions that are outgrown or outworn. If you have a clearout only once in a blue moon, you can expect your children to find the whole process much more invasive and difficult to accept.

Items to review

Children's belongings become redundant for many reasons. The most basic is that they are outgrown – either physically or in a developmental sense. A six-piece jigsaw is ripe for disposal when your child is happily tackling twenty-piece puzzles, just as booties are no longer required once she is wearing shoes.

Worn-out or outgrown clothing

In the early years, when children are growing rapidly, you will need to review their clothing every few months. Very young children often outgrow their clothes well before they are the worse for wear, so this is a stage when accepting hand-me-downs and passing your own child's clothes on to a friend or relative makes sense. If you are saving clothes to pass on, make you do so in good time or they may no longer fit. If you are keeping clothes to hand down to a sibling, put them in deep storage, protected against moths, dust and fading.

Outgrown toys, games and books

A degree of sensitivity and diplomacy is needed when you are tackling these categories of belongings. Accept that your children will have their own views on what they are prepared to part with and when, even if you consider the items in question to be too young for them.

Many children cling on to some of their soft toy favourites, picture books and old games well into the teenage years – and even beyond. This is not surprising. Treasured toys are part of a child's identity and should never be disposed of without their permission. You can appeal to your child's better nature by suggesting that their old toys, books, videos and games will find a worthy home and loving use when they are passed on to a younger relative, or to a hospital, clinic, school or charity. And you can always appeal to their acquisitive natures by explaining that freeing up shelf space will give them places to put their burgeoning collection of CDs and computer games.

Redundant equipment and accessories

Like adults, children often go through short-lived enthusiasms for particular sports or pastimes – skateboarding, ballet dancing, trumpet-playing, learning magic tricks, and so on. When the enthusiasm fades, in days, weeks or months, you might find yourself providing houseroom for the attendant clutter. You can make things easier (and more economic) for yourself by hiring or borrowing equipment until it is clear whether or not the activity will still retain its appeal once the initial flush of excitement has worn off. Hanging on to such items when the activity is no longer pursued is not simply a waste of space, but also serves to remind your child that he or she has not made the grade in some way. If your child can't get a note out of the clarinet, but is a whizz on the computer, don't keep the instrument hanging around where it will serve as a source of guilt and a reminder of failure.

Seasonal rotation

This strategy makes just as good sense for children's belongings as it does for adults'. Clothing and sports equipment can be rotated in and out of deep storage on a twice-yearly basis (see page 169 for advice on storing clothes).

Non-essential paperwork

Many schools and after-school clubs and activities generate mountains of paperwork on a termly basis. Separate out the essential from the disposable at regular intervals.

ABOVE: Bed, desk and storage boxes interconnect in this attic bedroom, making good use of available space and awkward angles. The desk is positioned under the roof light to benefit from natural light.

ABOVE: Underbed storage boxes can be improvised from a number of different types of container. Cut-out handles make retrieval easier, and a lick of paint makes the entire effect look well considered.

RIGHT: A low-level plinth running the length of the wall provides a place to play with toys, while storage boxes are tucked underneath. The low bookshelf at child height keeps favourite picture books within easy reach.

LEFT: Less is never more for children. If you have space to spare, it can be well worth designating a room as a playroom where most of your children's toys and games can be kept. Once toys have been abandoned in favour of computer games, the room can be updated into a home media centre.

OPPOSITE: Simple and accessible clothes storage encourages children to look after their clothes. A dash of colour adds to the appeal.

Care and maintenance

Family life is demanding enough without giving yourself extra chores in the way of housework. Choose surfaces and decorative finishes that can withstand a degree of punishment and can be cleaned and mopped easily. In the early years, make sure that messy play involving paints, clay and model-making takes place only in supervised areas that are easy to clean up, which more often than not will be the kitchen. Washable loose covers are a good idea for sofas and chairs. Paintwork that can be wiped down is a better wall treatment than paper and is easier to renew; a wall painted with blackboard paint provides a contained outlet for creativity.

Pay particular attention to flooring. In children's rooms floors should be warm and resilient for floor-based play. Cork, rubber and lino are relatively indestructible. Carpet helps to keep sound levels down, but you will need to guard against stains and accidental spills.

Safety tips:

• Keep all toxic substances under lock and key. These include bleaches, detergents and all other household cleaners; paints, sealants, varnishes and all types of glue; garden products such as insecticides, fertilizers and lawn dressings; prescription medicines and other remedies.

• Keep the first-aid box in a dedicated location where you can put your hands on it immediately in a crisis. Periodically check that it is well stocked and that nothing in it is out of date.

• All tall and heavy items of storage furniture should be anchored or bracketed securely against the wall to prevent them from toppling or being pulled over.

• Make sure that bunk beds or high-level beds are robustly made and conform with safety standards.

• Avoid glass doors or unit fronts at a low level where children might accidentally crash into them.

STORAGE SOLUTIONS FOR CHILDREN'S ROOMS

ABOVE: Containers really come into their own when it comes to organizing children's belongings. These colourful plaited plastic baskets are robust, versatile and cheerful. **BELOW LEFT AND CENTRE:** An ingenious, dual-purpose design marries covered storage bins on castors with a bench seat; the tough canvas cover can simply be unfastened to give access to the toys inside. **BELOW RIGHT:** The plastic stacking box is a storage standby and is ideal for playrooms.

ABOVE LEFT: Flat lidded plastic containers are ideal for underbed storage and can be used to house everything from shoes to toys to art materials. **ABOVE RIGHT:** Soft padded fabric containers are a good addition to the nursery. **BELOW LEFT:** These colour-coded catch-alls would be an excellent way of sorting one child's toys from another's. **BELOW RIGHT:** An improvised clothes rail made from a length of painted dowel suspended from cup hooks by coloured ribbons.

LEFT: The interior of this full-size wardrobe has been customized to suit the age of the child, with containers and racks underneath the hanging space.

ABOVE Spare blankets are kept in a lidded plastic container that slides neatly under a spare bed. Ideal for sleepovers, this bed doubles as a seating area and can also be slotted under the high-level bed if desired.

RIGHT: High-level or bunk beds must be sturdy in construction, with safe access provided by a secure ladder. Guard rails may be necessary for quite some time.

CASE STUDY: BEDROOM

Children's possessions are rarely accommodated using one type of storage system alone. For a start, most children like at least some of their belongings out on view or readily accessible on open shelves, where they can see them and derive pleasure and reassurance from ownership, as well as being able to reach with ease whatever book or toy they want at any given time. Then there is the fact that a child's room is a world in miniature, where many different types of things are kept – not merely clothing, as in adults' bedrooms, but toys, games, sports equipment, art supplies, and so on. A flexible blend of storage furniture, shelving, containers and display areas will be required to keep pace with the burgeoning belongings of the growing child.

In this girl's bedroom, a robust high-level bed makes the most of available floor area. Young children spend a lot of time playing on the floor and, as soon as they are old enough for such an arrangement to be safe, raised beds can be a practical option. In addition, as the child grows the space underneath that was used as a play area can be converted into storage, or a seating or study area. Equally practical and flexible is the full-size wardrobe. Until the child is older and requires full-length hanging space, the area under the rail usefully serves to house shoes and storage containers. Plastic lidded containers provide space for storing spare bed linen, while low-level modular shelving gives easy access to picture books and toys, and can be reconfigured as needs change.

all balloon cat can dog day daddy egg emmy for from frog go gate hat help his ice igloo ink jar kite lollipop

8. Working Areas

With the exception of home offices, many working areas in the home are behind the scenes and out of public view. Laundry and utility rooms, workshops, sheds, airing cupboards and linen rooms, for example, are functional places first and foremost, and tend not to feature in the house tour you give your guests. However, while such working areas may be a little basic when it comes to design and decoration, they do require careful planning to serve their purposes efficiently. Good systems of storage are an important part of tackling any task effectively – or in the case of a home business, profitably.

OPPOSITE: A home office may simply be where you tackle household accounts and routine admin. If you are earning your living from home, however, you need enough space to work effectively, as well as storage systems to support that work. These reclaimed wooden filing cabinets have great charm.

ASSESSING YOUR NEEDS

Many working areas are tucked away out of the main run of the household, so there is a tendency for them to silt up with possessions or equipment that have little relevance to the activity carried out there. Once your utility room was neat and tidy. Now, along with the washer, dryer and laundry basket, there is the ladder you used to change the light bulb in the kitchen that hasn't found its way back into the broom cupboard, bags of charcoal for the barbecue that haven't made it to the garage or shed, a box of old football boots you are saving for your nephew, bulk supplies of dog food … and what used to be a well-organized place to tackle the weekly wash is a cluttered space in which you can hardly move.

Whether it is the utility room, garage, shed or home workshop, all too often working areas become dumping grounds. A good starting point is to clear out all the clutter that doesn't really belong there and think carefully about where else such items should go or whether they merit being kept at all. Don't use working areas as places of deep storage unless you really have no alternative. In the same way, don't use working areas as holding places for equipment awaiting repair. Anything that has been sitting around for weeks or months while you find the spare time to fix it should be disposed of without delay.

In some households, working areas often say more about the people we think we should be than the people we really are. Unless you are keen and experienced at do-it-yourself, there is not much

point giving over a substantial area to tool storage. One recently published statistic showed that an electric drill sees no more than fifteen minutes of use during the average person's lifetime. If you are not particularly handy about the home, consider borrowing or hiring tools for the rare occasions when the spirit moves you to put up a shelf or hang a few pictures. Similarly, if you hate gardening, why not pay someone else to do routine maintenance for you, or commission a garden design that requires minimal upkeep with only a few basic tools?

Think about the way you allocate space. If your utility room is the only place you have available to store tools, garden equipment and other bulky items, but you have a generous family bathroom, it may be worth moving the laundry machines into the bathroom

ABOVE: A degree of separation from the rest of the household is important if you are working from home on a regular basis. Converted attics can make good home offices, with the area under the eaves providing ample storage space for files and other reference material.

RIGHT: Whatever storage system you adopt for working areas will depend on the nature of the work itself. For creative endeavours, you will need space for materials, tools and supplies, as well as places to keep finished work or completed orders.

LEFT: A back hallway has been transformed into a home office by lining one wall with a combination of shelving and drawer space under the worktop. When space is as tight as this, good organization is even more critical.

BELOW: Old metal containers have a certain well-worn appeal.

altogether. Alternatively, if you are very pressed for storage space indoors, there are many affordable sheds and outbuildings on the market that can provide a useful home for a whole range of equipment and supplies.

What to get rid of:

• Redundant tools. Many people find it difficult to dispose of tools because they are by their very nature useful items. But if you can't remember the last time you used the saw, it doesn't belong in your home; it belongs in the home of someone who enjoys woodworking.

• Old or duplicate tools and equipment. Old tools often find their way into our homes in the form of gifts or hand-me-downs. Don't keep duplicate tools – keep the newest and most effective, and get rid of the old garden fork that has lost half of its tines. In the same way, as soon as you replace an appliance such as a vacuum cleaner, get rid of the previous model. If you have upgraded and your old vacuum cleaner still has life in it, donate it to someone who can make use of it. Alternatively, there are charities that will take small appliances, check them over and offer them for sale at vastly reduced prices to people on low incomes.

• Dispose of guarantees, manuals and other types of paperwork relating to equipment or appliances that you have since replaced.

• Get rid of any supplies or equipment relating to hobbies that you no longer pursue. Donate or sell what is usable.

• Old decorating materials. Many people hang on to half-finished cans of paint, varnish and other decorating supplies. Rarely are these stored in such a way as to make the contents usable at a later date. Many of these chemical products pose a fire hazard and should be safely disposed of in an appropriate way. Consult your local council.

• Keep an eye on the contents of your linen or airing cupboard, and periodically weed out frayed towels, facecloths, bed linen, napkins and tablecloths. Many old towels make good all-purpose household cleaning cloths when they are too worn to be used in the bathroom. Threadbare sheets can do duty as dustsheets for decorating.

• Outdated paperwork and files. Paperwork relating to home businesses is a topic in itself (see pages 204–7), but usual household bills and accounts will require sifting through on a regular basis to prevent your in-tray from turning into an archive of the past ten years.

ABOVE: The way you arrange your working area should, to a large extent, echo the working process. Tools or equipment you use every day should be kept close at hand.
RIGHT: An efficient yet compact workstation in a cupboard. The keyboard is positioned on a sliding tray at the right ergonomic height to prevent wrist strain.

STORAGE STRATEGIES

Because working areas are out of public view, you don't have to worry about appearance and fine finishes when it comes to storage systems, containers or furniture. Concentrate, instead, on selecting items on the basis of practicality and robustness. Industrial or commercial storage systems are excellent for working areas in the home because they tend to be both strong and inexpensive. Some companies produce storage systems that are especially designed for garage or workshop use.

When you are planning storage for working areas, break down the sequence of activities in a logical fashion and arrange your tools, equipment and supplies accordingly. Certain of these will need to be kept in close proximity to where they will be used and others, particularly bulk supplies, can be stored a little out of the way. Segregate tools and equipment according to function, so that the garden tools, for example, are not muddled up with the tools you use for car maintenance.

Don't forget to light working areas to appropriately. A central ceiling light is adequate for a laundry or utility room, but you will need more targeted task lighting in an area that you are using for concentrated work at a bench, for example, or where you will be using power tools or sharp implements. A row of spotlights above a workbench may be the answer, or a basic Anglepoise for close desk-based work.

Types of storage

Fitted or built-in storage, which is so unobtrusive elsewhere in the home, is not necessary in working areas. Racks, shelves and containers serve most storage needs.

Hanging and racking systems

Make use of wall space by hanging or racking tools, equipment and materials. You can buy special perforated boards and suspend tools from individual hooks or brackets, or rig up your own racking system using lengths of timber or rails. Drawing or painting the outline of the tool on the wall or board will enable you to see at a glance what is missing.

Overhead drying racks can also be used to suspend a variety of articles apart from laundry. Stout brackets securely anchored

OPPOSITE: Borrow an old trick from pre-school – painting the outlines of tools on the wall lets you see at a glance where each belongs and which have gone astray.
RIGHT: Garden tools are often best hung up on wall racks or using some improvised arrangement of your own. Handles get into a tangle if you simply prop tools against the wall.

to the wall provide a good means of storing bicycles, lawnmowers and other bulky equipment. If your storage space is limited, keep the floor clear as far as possible.

Shelving

Bracketed shelving systems can house an inordinate amount of clutter in an organized fashion. You can vary the height and depth of the shelves to suit what you are storing. Freestanding industrial and commercial metal shelving units provide a good alternative to built-in shelves and can bear much heavier weights.

Containers

Use a selection of containers of different sizes to sort and store similar items. Don't be tempted to use containers as catch-alls or you will find yourself emptying them completely when you

are searching for a particular item. Keep nails and screws of different sizes and types in separate jam (jelly) jars or similar small containers. Label all of your containers so you know what is inside. Toolboxes that have interior compartments and tiered trays are also useful.

Locked cupboards

Any product or supply that is toxic should be kept under lock and key, particularly if there are children in the home. These include:

• Decorating materials, such as chemical strippers, paints, wood stains, varnishes, fillers, sealants, and so on.
• Garden products such as pesticide, lawn food and weed killer.
• Oil, lubricants, petrol and other types of fuel.
• Bleaches and cleansers.

LEFT: A well-ordered linen cupboard allows you to rotate sheets and towels so that all of your linen sees equal wear.

BELOW LEFT: Baskets make excellent containers for laundry, as they allow linen to be aired.

BELOW CENTRE: A utility room in a closet includes the washing machine, shelving for linen and a pull-out ironing board.

BELOW RIGHT: Racks and wire baskets attached to the back of the broom closet hold everything from the iron and ironing board to a squeegee and household cleansers.

LAUNDRY ROOMS AND UTILITY AREAS

If you have enough space in your home, an entire room devoted to doing the laundry can help take the drudgery out of this routine chore. Ideally, the room should be big enough for appliances, clothes baskets, detergents and other supplies, as well providing enough floor area to set up an ironing board.

It can also be useful if you store other household cleaning equipment, such a vacuum cleaners, floor mops and buckets, in the same place. It is best, however, if you do not keep do-it-yourself and garden tools in the same area, as you will run the risk of soiling clean laundry with grass cuttings, dirt and grease.

If you are short of space, you can site your laundry appliances in the kitchen or bathroom. Make sure that the area is well ventilated to prevent excess heat and humidity from building up. Washers and dryers can be stacked vertically if there is limited floor area. Ironing boards that are hinged to the wall or ones that pull out from under a worktop or counter are also space-saving.

Laundry bags or baskets should ideally be made of canvas, wickerwork or some other material that allows fabric to breathe. It can be useful to provide two separate baskets for dirty clothes, so that washing can be sorted straight away into whites and colours.

Linen storage and airing cupboards

Household linen – sheets, duvet covers, pillow cases and towels – should be stored together in a location that is warm, dry and accessible to both bedrooms and bathrooms. A common location for linen storage is the airing cupboard where the hot-water cylinder is located. Slatted shelves above the cylinder allow warm air to rise and dry any articles that are slightly damp. Ideally, the door of the cupboard should be pierced top and bottom with ventilation holes. If you do not have an airing cupboard, you can store linen in a separate closet, or in a chest, chest of drawers or armoire.

In many households linen cupboards have a tendency to be no-go areas. Damp or dirty towels are plucked off the bathroom floor and sheets are stripped from beds and go straight into the wash. Afterwards, the towels go back into circulation and beds are remade. The result of this approach is that linen wears unevenly, and most of what the linen cupboard contains is never used. You should aim to adapt your washing routine and organize your linen storage so that linens are used in rotation. Either separate flat sheets from contoured, duvet covers from pillow cases and always make up beds using the item from the bottom of the pile, or arrange linen in complete sets. The same strategy can be adopted for towels.

If you have enough space, bulky sweaters can be stored in the linen cupboard, too. Spare duvets and pillows, however, devour cupboard space and should be housed elsewhere in trunks or chests in the attic, or on upper shelves in a closet. Keep linen smelling fresh with lavender sachets or bags. If you are storing blankets and other woollen throws in the linen cupboard, make sure you add moth repellent.

HOME OFFICE

How you organize your home office will depend on the nature of the work that you carry out and whether or not your livelihood depends upon it. If you are earning your living from home, you need a dedicated area that provides you with the right conditions for concentrated, distraction-free work. However, even routine household administration requires a certain degree of organization if you are to keep ahead of the game.

Choose an area in your home that offers an element of physical and psychological separation from the rest of the household. For paying bills and keeping track of family schedules, a desk or worktable in the kitchen is often a good idea. Kitchens increasingly serve as family nerve centres these days.

Home offices and businesses, however, require a greater degree of separation, which means co-opting a spare or under-used room or part of a living area, converting an attic, or siting a workspace in an outbuilding such as a shed. Sheds, once an exclusively masculine domain, are proving increasingly popular with women who work at home. Companies that are addressing this trend market designs that come complete with electrical connections, interior fittings and insulation. Separate access to a working area is advisable if you regularly see clients at home.

If at all possible, try to plan ahead and anticipate how your needs might change in the future. Your fledgling home business might start small and need only limited space at the outset; future expansion, however, will demand greater accommodation. Any flexibility you can build in at the start in this regard will be welcome.

Storage strategies

As with any other space in the home, working areas require three levels of storage. Even if your work is not paper- or computer-based, the same basic approach holds. Items used everyday, such as appointment books, calendars, paperwork requiring immediate action and essential equipment, need to be kept on or near the worksurface or desktop. Otherwise, keep your worktop or desktop as clear as possible so that you can concentrate properly on the job in hand. Supplies that you use regularly, along with files, reference material or items relating to work in progress, should be stored close at hand, in filing cabinets, desk drawers, shelves over the desk or similar locations. Archives relating to your career history, including tax returns and similar documents, do not need to be in your working area at all.

• Second-hand office furniture and equipment is widely available. Basic items such as filing cabinets, office chairs that provide proper support for your back, lockers and cabinets, tables

ABOVE: Increasingly, kitchens are family nerve centres, and it makes sense to set aside an area for paying bills, keeping track of appointments and schedules and tackling other routine matters.
ABOVE RIGHT: This generous gallery and landing has been transformed into a library/working area, with bookcases lining one wall and an area for quiet study.
RIGHT: Good natural light and slightly more floor area than is standard makes this landing suitable for a home office.

and desks are all good purchases. Many retailers offer ranges of furniture and equipment for home offices, although such pieces may not be as robust.

• Choose a means of organizing files and papers, and stick to it to make storage displays less obtrusive. A neat array of box files looks better than a disparate collection of different files and containers, particularly on open shelving.

• If your work is art- or craft-based, decant your supplies into containers, preferably those that are see-through so you can read the contents at a glance.

• Make sure you dispose of outdated or replaced equipment (and its packaging) when you upgrade. Computers are expensive investments, but if you have recently bought a new model, get rid of the previous one. It is just occupying valuable working space.

Organizing paperwork

Most of the work that is carried out at home involves paper to some degree, and it is incredibly easy for a daunting backlog to build up. If you are running a household, that paper will take the familiar form of bills, notices, letters and junk mail; if you are running a business, there will be invoices, receipts and business correspondence to take into account. Added to which, many people keep hard paper copies of computer files on hand just in case of technical hitches. When your paperwork is threatening to turn into a never-ending a paper trail, it is time to get to grips with it.

• Immediately discard envelopes, inserts, promotional literature, junk mail and anything else that falls through the letterbox that you do not need to keep or reply to.

• Don't open your mail, then leave letters lying around in the hall, living room or bedroom. Make sure that you take each day's mail to the place where you usually deal with it.

• Separate important items that require a response, such as bills or urgent correspondence, from documents that need to be filed, such as insurance schedules. Put the former in your in-tray, and file the latter in an accessible location at one remove from your main working area.

• Separate household correspondence and paperwork from that relating to any professional work that you do at home. Set up dedicated files for bank and credit card business, insurance, your car, personal documents such as birth certificates and your children's school reports and examination certificates.

• It can be useful to keep a notebook on hand where you can jot down names and addresses of tradespeople or other useful contacts. Many people hang on to bits of paper simply because they serve as a record of addresses and phone numbers.

OPPOSITE AND RIGHT: When it comes to organizing your paperwork, reference material and other routine administrative details, it is important to keep like with like, so that your household accounts, for example, are not muddled up with your business receipts, and your children's school notices are not interleaved with work in progress.

• Discard all catalogues and other types of trade literature that are more than a year old.

• Set aside some time to periodically review any files relating to your working history. Once a project is completed, you do not need to keep every single piece of paper documenting its progress. Restrict immediate filing to documents going back no further than two years. Older files should go into deep storage if they contain documents that you need to keep for legal or tax purposes.

• Use a paper shredder to dispose of any documents or bills that could be used in identity theft.

Digital storage

Computers crash and sometimes, unfortunately, they die. At such times of crisis, your friendly computer technician may be able to retrieve your files from your hard disk – or not. Spare yourself the agony and make sure you back up your files regularly, on a daily basis if necessary.

Advances are made in methods of digital storage all the time. Depending on your computer, you can back up to disk, CD or DVD, or you may wish to invest in an external hard drive if you have large files to store. Memory sticks are another good means of storing data, particularly if you work on different computers in different locations and regularly transfer files back and forth.

STORAGE SOLUTIONS
FOR
WORKING SPACES

ABOVE: A contemporary variant on the traditional writing desk features open pigeonholes vividly accentuated with colour. **BELOW LEFT:** This neat wall-hung racking system allows you to suspend various accessories and containers to organize stationery and other office supplies. **BELOW RIGHT:** A mobile home-office trolley on castors opens out to reveal suspension files and shelves for storing documents, disks and other work-related items.

ABOVE LEFT: It is always useful to provide two laundry baskets so that dirty clothes can be immediately sorted into whites and colours. **ABOVE RIGHT:** This tiered clothes dryer is designed for pegging up socks and other small items. **BELOW LEFT:** Keep catalogues and other reference material in magazine racks.
BELOW RIGHT: Containers and box files are mainstays of home-office storage. Choose one particular style of container for the sake of visual consistency.

LEFT: A plastic pocketed wall-mounted storage panel provides room to keep everyday essentials.
OPPOSITE: The view of the workroom down the garden path. The path is made out of railway sleepers. Semi-tropical plants, including bamboo and banana, serve to create a visual screen.

CASE STUDY: WORKROOM

More and more people who work from home are finding that the humble garden shed satisfies many of their fundamental requirements for peace and quiet, psychological separation from the rest of the household and that pleasing sense of domain or territory which is so useful for concentrated or creative work. In recent years, the shed has cast aside its image as an exclusively male retreat, a place for a little time-wasting pottering, and found a new role as an affordable home-office option.

With a bit of time and effort you can upgrade an existing outbuilding or shed so that it provides proper conditions for working. Alternatively, there are ready-made sheds on the market designed expressly for home-office use. These generally come insulated and with electrical connections installed; the aesthetic, too, is often more upmarket beach hut than rough-and-ready

lean-to. In most cases, you will not need planning permission to site a shed in your garden, but it may be worth contacting your local planning officer to make sure that there are no restrictions with respect to siting.

This particular shed, situated at the bottom of the garden of a London townhouse, has seen several different manifestations. The former owner of the property, who was a rock musician, used it as a recording studio; the present owner, who runs a number of businesses connected with food, including a deli, a diner and a restaurant, now uses it as the base for his operations. Before he decided to work from home, however, he used the shed as a bar, with Guinness on tap.

The structure of the shed consists of concrete blocks, with a steel frame supporting a glass roof. The present owner installed

timber cladding to give the shed more of the feel of a rustic cabin; the flooring is terracotta tile. There is a wood-burning stove to supply warmth in winter; while the glass roof does mean that the workroom heats up a bit in summer, it is well ventilated. When the present owner decided to use the shed as his office, he had more electricity cables and telephone lines installed to support computers and other equipment.

The workroom interior is fitted out with a combination of mass-market basics – the worksurfaces – and high-quality flexible shelving. The workroom is square and measures 3.7 x 3.7m (12 x 12ft); accordingly, the arrangement of the desk area in a T-shape allows for the greatest number of different working permutations and makes it easy for several people to work at the same time. The pine walls are used as a message board and display area. The Universal shelving system, designed by Dieter Rams for Vitsoe, is expensive, but, like good pots and pans, it should last a lifetime.

The garden planting scheme was inspired by a trip to the Heligan in Cornwall, a garden that has been undergoing restoration for the past decade. Semi-tropical plants such as bamboo, tree ferns, gunnera and banana have been allowed to grow up into a jungle of greenery that slightly obscures the view – both of the shed from the house and the house from the shed. The pathway is made out of railway sleepers. The shed is sited 18m (60ft) from the house – a distance great enough to make potential interrupters think twice about intruding, yet close enough to retain a sense of integration of work and family life.

RIGHT: The interior organization of the workroom is designed to be as versatile as possible, with the desk space arranged in a T-shape and a flexible shelving system housing files and work records.

Resources

ADVICE

American Institute of Architects (AIA)
1735 New York Ave, NW,
Washington, DC 20006, USA
T: 1-800-AIA-3837
www.aia.org

American Society of Interior Designers (ASID)
608 Massachusetts Ave, NE,
Des Plaines, IL 60016, USA
Toll-free: 800-743-ASHI
www.ashi.com

British Interior Design Association
1–4 Chelsea Harbour Design
Centre, Chelsea Harbour,
London SW10 0XE, UK
T: +44 (0)20 7349 0800
www.bida.org.uk
Publishes a list of members.

The Consumers Association
2 Marylebone Road, London
NWI 4DF, UK
T: +44 (0)20 7770 7000
www.which.net

Federation of Master Builders
Gordon Fisher House,
14–15 Great James Street,
London WC1N 3DP, UK
T: +44 (0)20 7242 7583
www.fmb.org.uk

Home Improvement Lenders Association
1625 Massachusetts Ave, NW,
Suite 601, Washington, DC
20036-2244, USA
T: +1 202-265-4435
Useful information on planning, financing and executing home improvement projects.

National Association of the Remodeling Industry (NARI)
780 Lee Street, Suite 200,
Des Plaines, IL 60016, USA
T: +1 847-298-9200
Resource for contractors and suppliers; tips and homeowner's guide.

National Kitchen & Bath Association
687 Willow Grove Street,
Hackettstown, NJ 07840, USA
T: +1 877-NKBA-PRO
www.nkba.org
Publishes directory of certified bathroom designers and industry guidelines.

Royal Institute of British Architects
66 Portland Place, London
W1N 4AD, UK
T: +44 (0)20 7580 5533
www.riba.org

GENERAL STORAGE NEEDS AND ONE-STOP SHOPS

Advance Furniture
2525 Elmwood Avenue,
Buffalo, NY 14217, USA
Toll-free: 800-477-2285
www.ContemporaryFurniture.com
Online furniture site specializing in contemporary and Scandinavian designs

Aram
110 Drury Lane, London
WC2B 5SG, UK
T: +44 (0)20 7557 7557
www.aram.co.uk
Contemporary furniture from leading designers.

California Closets
1000 Fourth Street, Suite 800,
San Rafael, CA 94901, USA
T: +1 415 256 8500
www.calclosets.com
Closets and storage solutions for bedrooms, home offices, garages, living rooms, kitchens and utility rooms. Consultation and design service.

Crate & Barrel
Toll-free: 800-967-6696 for
local retail store
www.crateandbarrel.com
Online shopping for furniture and kitchen accessories. Stores all around the US.

FurnitureFind.com
Toll-free: 800-362-7632
www.furniturefind.com
Online shopping with a huge selection of furniture in all categories, with resources section, information and tips.

Distinction Furniture
Bishops Park House, 25–29
Fulham High Street, London
SW6 3JH, UK
T: +44 (0)20 7731 3460
www.distinction-furniture.co.uk
Contemporary furniture and interiors.

EasyClosets.com
Toll-free: 1-800-910-0129
www.easyclosets.com
Storage solutions for chests, pantries and laundry rooms. Design your closet online and receive free design plan.

Habitat
196 Tottenham Court Road,
London W1T 7LG
T: +44 (0)20 7631 3880
Call +44 (0)845 601 0740 for
branches or visit the website
www.habitat.net
Contemporary storage furniture and accessories.

Hammacher Schlemmer
147 East 57th Street,
New York, NY 10022, USA
Toll-free: 800-321-1484
www.hammacher.com
Specialty store with online shopping. Home-care department has many storage-related products.

Heal's
The Heal's Building,
196 Tottenham Court Road,
London W1T 7LQ, UK
T: +44 (0)20 7636 1666 for
branches or visit the website
www.heals.co.uk
Contemporary storage furniture and accessories.

Homebase
T: +44 (0)845 077 8888 for
branches or visit the website
www.homebase.co.uk
*300 stores in the UK. Storage
furniture and accessories,
including containers and
underbed storage.*

Home Depot
Toll-free: 1-800-430-3376
www.homedepot.com
*Huge selection of home
products online. Stores
throughout the US.*

Home Focus Catalog
Toll-free: 1-800-221-6771
www.homefocuscatalog.com
*Extensive selection of
storage items for indoors
and outdoors. Shop online
or call for a catalogue.*

IKEA
255 North Circular Road,
London NW13 0QJ, UK
T: +44 (0)845 355 1141 for
branches or visit the website
www.ikea.co.uk
*Fitted kitchens and bathrooms,
all kinds of storage furniture
and fittings, containers and
other storage accessories.
Design service available.
Stores nationwide*

in the USA:
Toll-free: 1-800-434-4532
www.ikea.com

Magnet
T: +44 (0)1535 661133 for
branches around the UK
www.magnet.co.uk
*Fitted kitchens, appliances,
bathrooms, bedrooms and
home offices.*

MFI
www.mfi.co.uk
*Fitted kitchens, bathrobes
and bedrooms. Wide range
of styles from contemporary
to classic to country. Design
service available. Branches
around the UK.*

Muji
www.mujionline.com
www.muji.co.uk
*Shelving, storage furniture,
containers, home office,
laundry, utility. Japanese
'no-brand' goods. 15 stores
throughout the UK; 6 stores
in Paris; other outlets in
Norway and Sweden.*

Organize-Everything.com
Toll-free: 1-800-600-9817
www.organize-everything.com
*Organizers for closets and
every room in the house;
special kids' storage line.*

Pottery Barn
Toll-free: 1-888-779-5176
for stores across the US
www.potterybarn.com
*Storage furniture and
accessories.*

SCP
135–139 Curtain Road,
London EC2A 3BX, UK
T: +44 (0)20 7739 1869
www.scp.co.uk
*Contemporary shelving and
storage furniture.*

Stacks and Stacks
1045 Hensley Street,
Richmond, CA 94801, USA
Toll-free: 1-800-761-5222
www.stacksandstacks.com
*Shop online for closet
organizers, shelving, bookcases, entertainment centres,
desks and room dividers.*

Target
1000 Nicollet Mall,
Minneapolis, MN 55403, USA
T: +1 612-304-6073
www.target.com
*Popular chain for affordable
furniture and furnishings.*

The Conran Shop
Michelin House, 81 Fulham
Road, London SW3 6RD, UK
T: +44 (0)20 7589 7401 and
55 Marylebone High Street,
London W1U 5HS, UK
T: +44 (0)20 7723 2223
www.conran.com
*Contemporary storage
furniture and accessories.*

in the USA:
The Terence Conran Shop
Bridgemarket, 407 East 59th
Street, New York, NY 10022
T: 212 755 9079

**The General Trading
Company**
2 Symons Street, Sloane
Square, London SW3 2TJ, UK
T: +44 (0)20 7730 0411
www.general-trading.co.uk
Storage accessories.

The Holding Company
241–245 Kings Road,
London SW3 5EL, UK
T: +44 (0)20 7352 1600 and

8 Upper Borough Walls,
Bath BA1 1RG, UK
T: +44 (0)1225 421 221
www.theholdingcompany.co.uk
*Storage specialists with a wide
range of furniture, fittings,
containers and storage
accessories.*

twentytwentyone
274 Upper Street, London
N1 2UA, UK
T: +44 (0)20 7837 1900
www.twentytwentyone.com
*Vintage 20th-century design
furniture and modern reissues
of contemporary classics.*

KITCHENS
See also under **GENERAL
STORAGE NEEDS**

Bulthaup
37 Wigmore Street, London
W1U 1PP, UK
T: +44 (0)20 7495 3663
www.bulthaup.com
*High quality contemporary
fitted and unfitted kitchens.*

Interluebke
www.interluebke.com
*German kitchen manufacturer.
Check the website for products
as well as dealers worldwide.*

Johnny Grey
Fyning Copse, Fyning Lane,
Rogate, Petersfield, Hants
GU13 5DH, UK
T: +44 (0)1730 821 424
www.johnnygrey.com
*Contemporary kitchens;
bespoke service available
in the UK and US.*

John Lewis of Hungerford
Park Street, Hungerford,
Berks RG17 0EF, UK
T: +44 (0)1488 688 100
www.john-lewis.co.uk
Bespoke classic kitchens.

Mirari
www.mirarikitchens.com
*International contemporary
kitchen design.*

Mowlem & Co
555 Kings Road, London
SW6 2EB, UK
T: +44 (0)20 7610 6626
www.mowlemandco.co.uk
Bespoke kitchens.

Plain English
The Tannery, Combs,
Stowmarket, Suffolk
IP14 2EN, UK
T: +44 (0)1449 774 028
www.plainenglishdesign.co.uk
Shaker-style kitchens.

Poggenpohl
Ransome Road, Far Cotton,
Northampton NN4 8AA, UK
T: +44 (0)1604 763 482 for
suppliers nationwide
www.poggenpohl.co.uk
Contemporary kitchens.

Shaker
72/73 Marylebone High
Street, London W1U 5JW, UK
T: +44 (0)20 7935 9461
www.shaker.co.uk
*Shaker-style kitchens and
other storage accessories.*

Siematic
www.siematic.com
*Contemporary kitchen
designs available worldwide.*

Smallbone
105–109 Fulham Road,
London SW3 6RL, UK
T: +44 (0)20 7581 9989
www.smallbone.co.uk
Classic kitchen designs.

Viaduct
1/10 Summer's Street,
London EC1R 5BD, UK
T: +44 (0)20 7278 8456
www.viaduct.co.uk
Contemporary designs.

BATHROOMS
See also under **GENERAL
STORAGE NEEDS**

Agape
via Po Barna, 69,
46031 Correggio Micheli di
Bagnola, San Vito, Milan, Italy
T: + 39 (0)376 250 311
www.agapedesign.it
*Bathroom products and
accessories.*

Alternative Plans
9 Hester Road, London
SW11 4AN, UK
T: +44 (0)20 7228 6460
www.alternative-plans.co.uk
*Bathroom products, fixtures
and accessories.*

Armitage Shanks
Rugeley, Staffordshire
WS15 4BT, UK
T: +44 (0)154 349 0253
www.armitage-shanks.co.uk
Suppliers nationwide.

Aston Matthews
141–147a Essex Road,
London N1 2SN, UK
T: +44 (0)20 7226 7220
www.astonmatthews.co.uk
*Contemporary and traditional
bathrooms and accessories.*

Avante Bathroom Products
Thistle House, Thistle Way,
Gildersome Spur, Wakefield
Road, Moreley, Leeds
LS27 7JZ, UK
T: +44 (0)113 201 2240
www.avantebathrooms.com

Bathaus
92 Brompton Road, London
SW3 1ER, UK
T: +44 (0)20 7225 7620
www.bathaus.co.uk

bathstore.com
T: 07000 228 478 for a
catalogue
www.bathstore.com
*Units, fixtures and
accessories; 87 branches
around the UK.*

Bed Bath and Beyond
Toll-free: 1-800-462-3966
www.bedbathandbeyond.com
Stores around the US.

Boffi
via Oberdan, 70-20030
Lentate sul Seveso,
Milan, Italy
T: + 39 (0)362 5341
www.boffi.com

Colourwash
Mail order: +44 (0)20 8944 6456
www.colourwash.co.uk
*Upmarket bathroom
specialists in the London area.*

C P Hart & Sons
Newnham Terrace, Hercules
Road, London SE1 7DR, UK
T: +44 (0)20 7902 1000
For branches around the UK.

Dornbracht
Köbbingser Mühle 6, D-58640
Iserlohn, Germany
T: +49 (0)2371 433 0
www.dornbracht.com

Duravit
Werderstrasse 36
78132 Hornberg
Germany
T: +49 (0)783 370 0
export@duravit.de

Duravit USA, Inc
1750 Breckinridge Parkway,
Suite 500, Duluth, GA 30096,
USA
T: 1-770-931-3575
Toll-free: 888-387-2848
info@usa.duravit.com

Ideal Standard
The Bathroom Works,
National Avenue, Hull
HU5 4HS, UK
T: +44 (0)1482 346 461
for suppliers nationwide
www.ideal-standard.co.uk

Original Bathrooms Ltd
143–145 Kew Road, Richmond,
Surrey TW9 2PN, UK
T: +44 (0)20 8940 7554

The White Company
8 Symons Street, London
SW3 2TJ, UK
T: +44 (0)20 7823 5322
Mail order: +44 (0)870 900 9555
www.thewhitecompany.com
*Bathroom storage and
accessories.*

Villeroy & Boch
Corporate Headquarters,
PO Box 1120, D 66688
Mettlach, Germany
T: + 49 (0)686 481 0 and
www.villeroy-boch.com
*Manufacturers of bathroom
products – range designed
by Conran & Partners.*

in the UK:
267 Merton Road, London
SW18 5JS, UK
T: +44 (0)208 871 4028

Waterworks
469 Broome Street, New
York, NY 10013, USA
T: +1 212-966-0605

BEDROOMS
See also under **GENERAL
STORAGE NEEDS**

Neville Johnson
Broadoak Business Park,
Ashburton Road West,
Trafford Park, Manchester
M17 1RW, UK
T: +44 (0)161 873 8333
www.nevillejohnson.co.uk
*Bespoke handcrafted
furniture. Specialists in
flexible space-saving furniture
and fittings, such as remote
controlled beds, concealed
study areas and integrated
entertainment storage. Multifunctional 24-hour flexible
room combines work area,
bed, wardrobe, entertainment
in one fitted solution.*

Cath Kidston
51 Marylebone Hight Street,
London W1U 5AW
T: 020 7935 6555
Mail order: 0870 850 1084
www.cathkidston.co.uk
*Pretty retro storage
accessories. Also kitchen
containers and stationery.
500 stockists worldwide,
2 US stores, 7 UK stores.*

Closet Valet
2033 Concourse Drive,
St Louis, MO 63146-4118, USA
Toll-free: 1-800-878-2033
www.closetvalet.com
*Specialty closet organizers
and accessories include built-
in ironing boards, valet closet
rods, belt racks and tie racks.*

**HOME OFFICES AND
WORK AREAS**
See also under **GENERAL
STORAGE NEEDS**

Brookstone
Toll-free: 1-800-846-3000
www.brookstone.com
*Exclusive hardware specialty
shop, selling storage solutions
for closets, kitchens, home
offices and garages.*

Createspace
T: +44 (0)1564 711 177
www.create-space.com
Extensions and garden rooms

Garden Lodges
T: +44 (0) 1582 896 596
www.gardenlodges.co.uk
Garden rooms and work areas.

Henley Offices
T: +44 (0)870 240 7490
www.henleyoffices.com
Garden workrooms and sheds.

HomeOfficeDirect.com
Toll-free: 877-709-9700
www.homeofficedirect.com

Home & Office Ltd
T: +44 (0)800 389 4753
www.homeandoffice.co.uk
Garden rooms and sheds.

Inside Out Buildings
T: +44 (0)1524 737 999
www.iobuild.co.uk
Garden rooms.

Knoll International
Toll-free: 800-343-5665
www.knoll.com
*High quality home office
furniture.*

Paperchase
www.paperchase.co.uk
*Design-led stationery. 71 UK
outlets, plus stores in US,
Australia and Singapore.*

Workbench
Toll-free: 800-736-0030
www.workbenchfurniture.com
*Modern furniture and storage
for home offices.*

**SALVAGE AND
DISPOSAL**

American Salvage
9200 NW 27th Ave, Miami,
FL 33147, USA
T: +1 305-836-4444
www.americansalvage.com

**Architectural Antiques
Exchange**
715 North Second Street,
Philadelphia, PA 19123, USA
T: +1 215-922-3669
www.architecturalantiques.com

LASSco
St Michael's, Mark Street,
London EC2A 4ER, USA
T: +44 (0)20 7749 9944
www.lassco.co.uk

**London Community
Recycling Network**
T: +44 (0)20 7324 4690
*Details of Appliance Reuse
Centres and Furniture Reuse
Network.*

Morph
www.morph.org.uk
*Shop selling donated
second-hand furniture
at affordable prices.*

www.swapxchange.org
*Exchange what you don't
want for what you do want.*

Salvage Web
www.salvageweb.com
*Online service for architectural
salvage exchange.*

Walcot Reclamation
108 Walcot Street, Bath
BA1 5BT, UK
T: +44 (0)1225 444 404
www.walcot.com

Index

Acknowledgments

The publisher would like to thank the following photographers, agencies and architects for their kind permission to reproduce the photographs in this book:

1 Mark Luscombe-Whyte/Grand Designs Magazine; 2 and 4 Chris Tubbs/Conran Octopus (T Conran); 5 Morley von Sternberg (Architect: Ab Rogers Design); 7 Yoshida Makoto/Architects: Yasuhiro Yamashita/Atelier Tekuto; 8 Tim Evan-Cook/Red Cover; 10–11 Ken Hayden/Red Cover (Architect: John Pawson); 12 Tom Mannion; 13 Ngoc Minh Ngo; 14 Stellan Herner (Stylist: Mikael Beckman); 17 Chris Tubbs/Conran Octopus (T Conran); 18 D Brandsma/S Houx/Sanoma Pictures; 21 D Chatz/Inside/Photozest; 23 Nathalie Krag/Taverne Agency (Stylist: Tami Christiansen); 25 Phil Aynsley; 27 Paul Lepreux/Marie Claire Maison (Stylist: Catherine Ardouin); 28 Jake Fitzjones/Living Etc/IPC Syndication; 29 Mark Scott/Woman & Home/IPC Syndication; 31 Nigel Rigden; 32 David Clerihew/Living Etc/IPC Syndication; 33 Eugeni Pons/RBA; 34 left Bill Kingston/Living Etc/IPC Syndication; 35 right P Grootes/Sanoma Pictures; 36 Ray Main/Mainstream; 37 left Ed Reeve/Red Cover; 37 right Paul Massey/Living Etc/IPC Syndication; 39 B Claessens/Inside/Photozest; 40 Jake Fitzjones/Living Etc/IPC Syndication; 41 Stellan Herner (Stylist: Gill Renlund); 42 Ingalill Snitt; 43 Winfried Heinze/Living Etc/IPC Syndication; 44 Chris Tubbs/Conran Octopus; 45 Chris Tubbs/Conran Octopus; 46 Hotze Eisma/Taverne Agency (Stylist: Rianne Landstra); 47 Ngoc Minh Ngo; 49 Damian Russell/Elle Decoration; 51 Lien Botha/Visi/Camera Press (Dedato designers and architects); 52 left Alun Callender/Woman & Home/IPC Syndication; 52 right Alexander van Berge/Taverne Agency/Elle Wonen; 53 left Harry Poortman (Dedato designers and architects); 53 right Warren Heath/H&L/Inside/Photozest; 54 Vercruysse & Dujardin (Designer & owner: Patrick Roelens); 55 Stefan Mueller-Naumann/artur; 55 below Amanda Turner/Red Cover; 57 Jason Lowe/Red Cover (Architect: Ken Shuttleworth); 58 Gianni Basso/Vega MG; 59 above left R Frinkling/A Brands/Sanoma Pictures; 59 above right Grant Scott/Elle Decoration; 59 below Iben Ahlberg/Home Sweet Home Co.; 60 Jake Curtis/Red Cover; 61 Stellan Herner (Architect: Max Holst/Sandell Sandberg); 62 left Mike Daines/Red Cover (Designer: Jo Warman); 62 right Simon Brown/Homes & Gardens/IPC Syndication; 63 Mark Munro (Designer: Robert Rolls/First Impressions Projects); 64 above Bertrand Limbour/Inside/Photozest; 64 below Mike Daines/Red Cover (Designer: Jo Warman); 65 Morley von Sternberg (Architect: Ab Rogers Design); 66 Vercruysse & Dujardin (Architect & owner: Karel Vandenhende); 67 left Nathalie Krag/Taverne Agency (Stylist: Tami Christiansen); 67 right Gianni Basso/Vega MG; 69 Mirella van Basten; 70 above Bjorg Magnea; 70 below Ignacio Martinez; 71 Hotze Eisma/Taverne Agency (Stylist: Tami Christiansen); 72 Alessandra Ianniello/Studio Pep; 73 Alexander van Berge/Taverne Agency/Ulrika Lundgren; 74 David Clerihew/Living Etc/IPC Syndication; 75 Kristian Septimius Krogh/House of Pictures; 77 Chris Tubbs/Conran Octopus (T Conran); 78 Gavin Kingcome (Designer: Suzannah Baker Smith); 79 left Andrew Wood/The Interior Archive (Designer: Peter Wylly/Babylon Design); 79 right Andrew Wood/The Interior Archive (Architect: Spencer Fung); 80 above Mark Luscombe-Whyte/The Interior Archive (Designer: Simon Finch); 80 below Stefen Clement/Stylist S Cardon/Inside/Photozest; 81 Alexander van Berge/Taverne Agency/Ulrika Lundgren; 82 Andreas von Einsiedel (Designer/owner: Kenyon Kramer); 83 David Ross/Visi/Camera Press (Architect: Thomas Gouws Architects; Stylist: Annemarie Meintjes); 84 Richard Powers (Architect: Andrew Lister); 87 Jan Verlinde; 89 Dan Duchars/Living Etc/IPC Syndication; 91 Ray Main/Mainstream; 93 left Nick Allen/Living Etc/IPC Syndication; 93 right Mads Mogensen(Stylist: Martina Hunglinger); 94 Jean Luc Laloux; 95 Alessandra Ianniello/Studio Pep; 97 left Chris Tubbs/Red Cover; 97 right Tomas Riehle/artur; 98 above Ray Main/Mainstream; 98 below Tuca Reines (Architect: Arthur Casas); 99 Ray Main/Mainstream; 101 Guy Obijn; 102 Jake Curtis/Living Etc/IPC Syndication; 103 Chris Tubbs/Conran Octopus; 104 Chris Tubbs/Conran Octopus (Stylist: Nicky Peters); 105 Ray Main/Mainstream (Architect: Kralform); 106 above right The Holding Company; 106 below left Twentytwentyone; 106 below right Heals; 107 above right The Holding Company; 107 above right Twentytwentyone; 107 below left and below right Thomas Stewart/Conran Octopus; 108–109 Erwin Nagel/Workshop of Wonders; 110–113 Chris Tubbs/Conran Octopus (T Conran); 115 Vercruysse & Dujardin (Designer & owner: Genevieve Marginet); 117 above left David Sandison; 117 above right Pia Ulin; 117 below right Jean Luc Laloux (Architect: V Van Duysen); 118 M Schets/Sanoma Pictures; 120 above Mai Linh/Marie Claire

Maison (Stylist: Catherine Ardouin); 120 below left Jan Baldwin/Narratives (Architects: MMM Architects); 120 below right Chris Tubbs/Conran Octopus; 121 Ed Reeve/Red Cover; 122 Guy Obijn (Interior Designer: Kristel Peeters); 123 Debi Treloar/Homes & Gardens/IPC Syndication; 123 right Chris Tubbs/Conran Octopus; 123 below left Giorgio Possenti/Vega MG (Architect: Bart Lens); 124 above Patrick Ansellem/Marie Claire Maison (Stylist: Catherine Ardouin); 124 below Simon Brown/Homes & Gardens/IPC Syndication; 125 Alberto Piovano/Arcaid (Architect: M Romanelli); 126 Chris Tubbs/Conran Octopus (Stylist: Nicky Peters); 128 left Ed Reeve/Red Cover; 128 right Gilles de Chabaneix/Stylist: Daniel Rozensztroch/Marie Claire Maison/Camera Press; 129 Chris Tubbs/Conran Octopus (Stylist: Nicky Peters); 130 Paul Zammit/Homes & Gardens/IPC Syndication; 131 Chris Tubbs/Conran Octopus (T Conran); 132 Douglas Gibb/Red Cover; 133 above Andreas von Einsiedel (Designer/owner: Anne Millais); 133 below Chris Tubbs/Conran Octopus (T Conran); 134 Stefen Clement/Stylist M Radot/Inside/Photozest; 135 Alessandra Ianniello/Studio Pep; 136 above right Mowlem & Co.; 136 below left Interlübke; 136 below centre Ikea; 136 below right John Lewis; 137 above left Habitat; 137 above right Siematic; 137 below left and below centre Mirari Kitchens; 137 below right The Holding Company; 138–139 Andreas von Einsiedel (Designer & owner: Jasper Conran); 140 Andreas von Einsiedel (Designer & owner: Jasper Conran); 142 left Ray Main/Mainstream (Architect: Julie Richards); 143 right David Sandison; 145 left D Brandsma/Sanoma Pictures ; 145 above right Paul Graham/Living Etc/IPC Syndication; 145 below right Hotze Eisma/Taverne Agency (Stylist: Tatjana Quax); 146 Jake Fitzjones; 148 above left Chris Tubbs/Conran Octopus (T Conran); 148 above right Alessandra Ianniello/Studio Pep; 148 below Verne Fotografie; 149 left Andreas von Einsiedel (Designer & owner: Fiona Adamczewski); 149 right P Kooijman/Sanoma Pictures; 149 centre Hotze Eisma/Taverne Agency (Stylist: Reina Smit); 150 above Andreas von Einsiedel (Designer & owner: Avril Delahunty); 150 below Ray Main/Mainstream; 151 Marie-Pierre Morel/Marie Claire Maison (Stylist: Daniel Rozensztroch); 152 above Baileys Home and Garden; 152 below left and right Colourwash; 153 above left and centre Baileys Home and Garden; 153 above right John Lewis; 153 below left Boffi; 153 below right The Holding Company; 154 Patrice de Grandry/Madame Figaro/Camera Press; 157 Grant Scott/Living Etc/IPC Syndication; 158 left Scott Frances (Architect: Stephen Roberts); 158 right Daniel Hertzell; 160 above Edina van der Wyck/The Interior Archive (Designer: Atlanta Bartlett); 160 below L Wauman/Inside/Photozest; 162 left Bob Smith/Living Etc/IPC Syndication; 162 right Karin Björkquist (Stylist: Jacob Solgren, Architect: Per Söderberg); 163 left Paul Lepreux/Marie Claire Maison (Stylist: Gael Reyre); 163 right Andreas von Einsiedel (Designer & owner: Eugenie Voorhees); 164 above Andreas Mikkel (Stylist: Andrea Larsson); 164 below left Douglas Gibb/Red Cover; 164 below centre Daniel Hertzell; 164 below right Brett Boardman (Architect: Drew Heath); 165 Gavin Kingcome (Designer: Suzannah Baker Smith); 166 Henry Wilson/Red Cover (Architect: Ian Chee & Voon Wong Lee of VX; Designer: Florence Lim); 167 above Guy Obijn (Interior Designer: Paul Linse); 167 below left Chris Tubbs/Conran Octopus; 167 below right Jean Luc Laloux (Architect: P Hoet-Instore); 168 James Silverman (Architect: Gert Wingårdh/Wingårds; Owner: Gunnela and Johan Dieden); 169 Jake Fitzjones/Red Cover (Designer: Richard Muddirr Design); 170 above right The White Company; 170 below left The Holding Company; 170 below right F Amiand/Stylist: Oddes/Postic/Marie Claire Maison/Camera Press; 171 above left and above right Aram Designs Ltd; 171 below left Ikea; 171 below right Distinction of Furniture; 172–173 Hotze Eisma (Stylist: Marielle Maessen); 175 Kate Gadsby/Narratives; 177 left Paul Massey/Mainstream; 177 right L Lemaire/Sanoma Pictures; 178 left Paul Lepreux/Marie Claire Maison (Stylist: Gael Reyre); 178 right James Morris/The Interior Archive (Architect: AHMM); 179 Ray Main/Mainstream; 181 Chris Tubbs/Conran Octopus; 182 left L Lemaire/Sanoma Pictures; 182 right Jefferson Smith/Grand Designs Magazine (Artist: Mark Surridge); 183 S de Geus/Sanoma Pictures; 184 Karin Björkquist (Stylist Jacob Solgren); 185 left Niels Harving & Lykke Foged; 185 right Stellan Herner (Stylist: Mikael beckman, Architect: Jordens Arkitekter); 186 Ray Main/Mainstream (Architect: Seth Stein Architects); 187 Amy Hall/Taverne Agency (Stylist: Tilly Hazenberg); 188 below left and below centre Verity Welstead/Conran Octopus; 188 below right Ikea; 189 above left The Holding Company; 189 above right and below left John Lewis; 189 below right Verity Welstead/Conran Octopus; 190–191 Chris Tubbs/Conran Octopus (Nicky Peters); 193 Antoine Rozes; 194 left E Huibers/Sanoma Pictures; 195 right Alexander van Berge/Taverne Agency/Ulrika Lundgren; 196 left Jake Curtis/Living Etc/IPC Syndication; 196 right Giorgio Possenti/Vega MG; 197 above E Huibers/Sanoma Pictures; 197 below B Brussee/Sanoma Pictures; 198 Jacqui Hurst; 199 and 200 above Chris Tubbs/Conran Octopus (T Conran); 200 below left Ray Main/Mainstream; 200 below centre Warren Heath/H&L/Inside/Photozest; 200 below right Andreas von Einsiedel (Designer/owner: Dominic Ash); 203 above left D Brandsma/Sanoma Pictures; 203 above right Luke White/The Interior Archive; 203 below Jean Luc Laloux (Architect: Bataille & Ibens); 204–205 Chris Tubbs/Conran Octopus (Nicky Peters); 206 Daniel Hertzell; 208 above right Twentytwentyone; 208 below left Knoll, inc.; 208 below right The Holding Company; 209 above left The Holding Company; 209 above right and below left Muji; 209 below right Winfried Heinze/Conran Octopus; 210–213 Chris Tubbs/Conran Octopus; 224 Nathalie Krag/Taverne Agency (Stylist: Tami Christiansen)

Every effort has been made to trace the copyright holders. We apologize in advance for any unintentional omissions and would be pleased to insert the appropriate acknowledgement in any subsequent publication.